Memoirs

of

Madame Vigée Lebrun

Memoirs

of

Madame Vigée Lebrun

Translated by
Lionel Strachey

Introduction by
John Russell

George Braziller, Inc., Publishers

The publisher would like to thank Mr. Joseph Baillio
of Wildenstein & Co., Inc., New York for his generous
assistance at various phases of this project.

Published in the United States of America in 1989
by George Braziller, Inc. Originally published in 1903
by Doubleday, Page and Company.

For information address the publisher :

George Braziller, Inc.
60 Madison Avenue
New York, New York 10010

Library of Congress Cataloging in Publication Data :

Vigée-Lebrun, Louise-Elisabeth, 1755–1842.
[Souvenirs, English]
Memoirs of Madame Vigée Lebrun / translated by
Lionel Strachey :
Introduction by John Russell.
p. cm.
Translation of : Souvenirs.
Originally published : New York : Doubleday, Page, 1903.
Includes index.

ISBN 0-8076-1221-9.—ISBN 0-8076-1222-7 (pbk.)

1. Vigée-Lebrun, Louise-Elisabeth, 1755–1842.   2. Painters—
France—Biography.   I. Title.
ND553.V5325A2   1989
759.4 — dc19
[B]   88-38757
CIP

Printed and bound in the United States
by Ray Freiman & Company.

PREFATORY NOTE

Madame Lebrun brought out her Memoirs at the suggestion of her friend, the Princess Dolgoruki, in 1835. The authoress was born in 1756, at Paris, where she died in 1842. She was the daughter of Louis Vigée, an obscure portrait painter. Her baptismal name was Marie Louise Élisabeth. In 1776 Mademoiselle Vigée was married to Jean Baptiste Pierre Lebrun, a notable picture dealer and critic, known also to his contemporaries as an inveterate gambler.

CONTENTS

CONTENTS

CONTENTS

CONTENTS

CONTENTS

LIST OF ILLUSTRATIONS

Front Cover:
Self-Portrait of the Artist with her Daughter, 1789.
The Louvre, Paris.

INTRODUCTION

Dr. Samuel Johnson believed that in the scale of human felicity it would be difficult to top the pleasure of "driving briskly in a post chaise with a pretty woman."

I wouldn't quarrel with that. But there are days when it's raining, and the horse has gone lame, and the pretty woman has something better to do. When that happens, I turn for the hundredth time to the memoirs of Madame Vigée Lebrun, and I am never disappointed.

This is a book that one can open at any time, and in any place, and be sure of enjoying oneself. It reads like the kind of conversation that one always hopes to hear but all too rarely does. In prose, as much as in paint, Madame Vigée Lebrun had a genius for portraiture. She lived for a very long time—from 1755 to 1842. She knew "everybody," from the last years of the *ancien régime*, through the years of the Revolution of 1789 and the ascendancy of Napoleon. Twelve years after the end of the Restoration and a mere six years before the risings of 1848, her life ended as fresh as when it began.

As much at home in England, Germany, Austria, Switzerland, and Russia as in her native France, she had a wonderful eye not only for human beings but for the way they lived and the way they got on (or sometimes did not get on) with one another. Not a detail of their houses, their gardens, their dress, or their family situation escaped her. Though she was discretion itself in re-

lation to her private affairs, she was particularly shrewd
at sizing up the entanglements of others. At ease in all
societies, she had perfect pitch in conversation and never
said a silly thing (or an ill-natured one).

Everywhere and at all times, people craved her company. They craved her portraits, too, and by her own
account she painted at least 660 of them during her long
career. They were a success from the very beginning. In-
evitably there were minor talents (and at least one major
one) who were envious of her. She must have known that
wherever she went she had the admiration of her colleagues and her peers.

It was fundamental to her success that she regarded
portrait painting as a conversational activity, a duet for
equals, in which the sitter, though never flattered, was
coaxed along as a human being. For that reason, her best
portraits have the character of a lively, unforced, and
never-betrayed confidential talk between painter and
sitter.

A true professional, she put her cosmopolitan experience to the best possible uses. (One of her more unex-
pected observations was that both Germans and
Austrians have their ears higher on the head than is cus-
tomary in any other part of Europe, thereby calling for
minor triumphs of adaptation on the painter's part.) In
all things, she was the champion of true feeling and
spontaneity and the enemy of formula.

In her "Advice to a Portrait Painter," one of the
best things of its kind ever written, she put the case for
easy and natural human exchange as the essential foun-
dation, without which no portrait was worth a damn. But
she also gave the minutest advice about how to handle
the head, the hair, the eyes, the nose, the cheeks, the

mouth, the jawbone, the neck, the collarbone, the elbow,
the kneecap, and the heel. Yet in her own work, all these
things seemed to flow from the brush without effort.

Her best portraits look like spring flowers with the
dew still on them. And it is precisely that quality that we
find in her memoirs. It might have been otherwise. She
lived in tumultuous times. Her marriage was a mess
from the beginning. Social, political, and military con-
vulsions were all around her. Without her gift for getting away in the nick of time, and for falling on her feet
in a new country with a whole slew of new friends and
admiring acquaintances, war and revolution might well
have had their way with her.

But if she was ever tired, lonely, bored, unwell, or on
the rack with anxiety, she never let us know about it. A
certain sainted innocence attended her even in situations
where most women lay their plans well in advance.
(When told one morning by her best friend that she
would undoubtedly give birth during the day, she said,
"Oh, no. I can't possibly do that. I have a sitter coming
tomorrow.")

Whining and recrimination were quite foreign to
her. Even though her husband stole all her earnings for
the best part of twenty years, she behaved as if it were a
minor failing of character. And when the painter
Jacques-Louis David pursued her with calumnious
hatred, she thought that he was really too childish for
her to take it seriously.

As for the great names of her day—among them
Talleyrand, Lord Byron, Catherine the Great of Russia,
Buffon the naturalist, Beaumarchais the dramatist, the
future King George IV of England, and Benjamin
Franklin, the favored guest of every salon in Paris—she

was the most reliable of witnesses. She was never pert. She never toadied. She never boasted. She knew the best actors, the best singers, the best writers, and the best painters of her time. As to her own attractions, she was modesty itself and said flatly and in some detail that in first youth she had been hideous. So when she tells us that Voltaire in his last days kissed her portrait over and over again, we believe her.

She spent almost nothing on her clothes, prided herself on always doing her own hair, and never tried to keep up with fashion, let alone to lead it. She was unfeignedly amazed when, quite early in her career, she was applauded by the entire audience when she went to the theater. And when she returned to Paris after the Revolution, she was amazed all over again that the actors of the Comédie Française should ask to come and perform in her drawing room, with the great dancer Madame Vestris as a supplementary attraction.

When heads of state stood in line, almost, to be painted by her, she treated them with exactly the same unaffected cordiality with which she treated everyone else. No one was ever less of a snob than Elisabeth Vigée Lebrun, and she was never swayed in the least by considerations of rank, or wealth, or power. But that she knew a fraud when she saw one is shown by her portrait in prose of Mesmer, the celebrated pseudo healer.

She loved a good story, and just occasionally she could not resist one that might have been too good to be true. One such concerns the occasion on which Talleyrand gave a dinner for Vivant Denon, a great esthete of the day who had lately been to Egypt with Napoleon. Talleyrand asked his wife to read aloud to him from Denon's writings, by way of preparation.

In her anxiety not to keep him waiting, Madame de Talleyrand pulled out a copy of *Robinson Crusoe* by mistake. Specimen pages found a ready hearing. When the time came for Talleyrand to address a word of welcome to Vivant Denon, he said how much he had enjoyed reading the story of his travels—"Above all, the moment at which you first came face to face with Man Friday."

But set pieces of that sort are rare in her memoirs, where the general tone is one of simplicity and straightforwardness, allied to rare powers of insight and observation. Madame Vigée Lebrun had none of the airs of the traditional "society portraitist." She would rather lunch on a boiled egg in her studio than go to a great house in hopes of drumming up trade. If she went to a country fête in Switzerland with Madame de Staël, she was more interested in the fête than in the fact that she was sitting next to one of the most famous women in Europe. Madame de Staël was fun, but so was the fête—and all the more so because it happened only once in every hundred years.

She was a woman of the world, in a sense that now has almost no meaning, but she was also a full-time, hard-working professional painter. It is the interaction between the two that makes her autobiography one of the most fascinating books of its kind. Reading it, we fall under her spell, and when we get to the end of it, we want nothing so much as to start all over again.

John Russell

Memoirs

of

Madame Vigée Lebrun

CHAPTER I

Youth

I WILL begin by speaking of my childhood, which is the symbol, so to say, of my whole life, since my love for painting declared itself in my earliest youth. I was sent to a boarding-school at the age of six, and remained there until I was eleven. During that time I scrawled on everything at all seasons; my copy-books, and even my schoolmates', I decorated with marginal drawings of heads, some full-face, others in profile; on the walls of the dormitory I drew faces and landscapes with coloured chalks. So it may easily be imagined how often I was condemned to bread and water. I made use of my leisure moments outdoors in tracing any figures on the ground that happened to come into my head. At seven or eight, I remember, I made a picture by lamplight of a man with a beard, which I have kept until this very day. When my father saw it he went into transports of joy, exclaiming, "You will be a painter, child, if ever there was one!"

3

I mention these facts to show what an inborn passion for the art I possessed. Nor has that passion ever diminished; it seems to me that it has even gone on growing with time, for to-day I feel under the spell of it as much as ever, and shall, I hope, until the hour of death. It is, indeed, to this divine passion that I owe, not only my fortune, but my felicity, because it has always been the means of bringing me together with the most delightful and most distinguished men and women in Europe. The recollection of all the notable people I have known often cheers me in times of solitude.

As a schoolgirl my health was frail, and therefore my parents would frequently come for me to take me to spend a few days with them. This, of course, suited my taste exactly. My father, Louis Vigée, made very good pastel drawings; he did some which would have been worthy of the famous Latour. My father allowed me to do some heads in that style, and, in fact, let me mess with his crayons all day. He was so wrapt up in his art that he occasionally did queer things from sheer absent-mindedness. I remember how, one day, after dressing for a dinner in town, he went out and almost immediately came back, it having occurred to him that he would like to touch up a picture recently begun. He removed his wig, put on a nightcap, and went out again in this head-gear, with his gilt-frogged coat, his sword, etc. Had not one of his neighbours stopped him, he would have exhibited himself in this costume all through the town.

He was a very witty man. His natural good spirits infected every one, and some came to be painted by him for the sake of his amusing conversation. Once, when he was making a portrait of a rather pretty woman, my father observed, while he worked at her mouth, that she made all manner of grimaces in order to make that organ look smaller. Falling out of patience with all this maneuvering, my father quietly remarked:

"Please don't let me give you so much trouble. You have only to say the word and I will paint you without a mouth."

My mother was an extremely handsome woman. This may be judged from the pastel portrait made of her by my father, as well as from my own oil painting of a much later date. She carried her goodness to austerity, and my father worshipped her as though she had been divine. She was very pious, and, in heart, I was so, too. We always heard high mass together, and were regular attendants at the other church services. Especially in Lent did we never omit any of the prescribed devotions, evening prayer not excepted. I have always liked sacred singing, and in those days organ music would often move me to tears.

My father was in the habit of inviting various artists and men of letters to his house of an evening. At the head of them I must place Doyen, the historical painter, my father's most intimate and my first friend. Doyen was the nicest man in the world, so clever and so good; his views on persons and things were always exceedingly just, and moreover he talked about painting with such fervent enthusiasm that it made my heart beat fast to listen to him. Poinsinet was very clever, too, and gay. Perhaps his extraordinary credulity is generally known. As a consequence of it he was continually made game of in the most unheard-of ways. Some friends once told him that there was an office called the King's Screen, and persuaded him to stand before a blazing fire so hot that it nearly roasted his calves. When he attempted to move away, he was told he must not stir, but that he must accustom himself to intense heat or he would not get the post. Poinsinet was, however, far from being a fool. Many of his works are still in favour, and he is the only author who ever gained three dramatic successes in one night:

"Ermeline," at the Grand Opéra; "The Circle," at the Théâtre Française; "Tom Jones," at the Opéra Comique. Some one put it into his head that he had a taste for travel, so he began with Spain, and was drowned while crossing the Guadalquivir.

I may also mention Davesne, painter and poet. He was rather mediocre in both arts, but was bidden to my father's suppers because of his witty conversation.

Though nothing more than a child, the jollity of these suppers was a great source of pleasure to me. I was obliged to leave the table before dessert, but from my room I heard the laughter and the joking and the songs. These, I confess, I did not understand; nevertheless, they helped to make my holidays delightful. At eleven I left the boarding-school for good, after my first communion. Davesne, who painted in oils, sent his wife for me to teach me how to mix colours. Their poverty grieved me deeply. One day, when I wanted to finish a head I had begun, they made me remain to dinner. The dinner consisted of soup and baked apples.

I was overjoyed at not having to leave my parents again. My brother, three years younger than I, was as lovely as an angel. I was not nearly so lively as he, and far from being so clever or so pretty. In fact, at that time of my life I was very plain. I had an enormous forehead, and eyes far too deep-set; my nose was the only good feature of my pale, skinny face. Besides, I was growing so fast that I could not hold myself up straight, and I bent like a willow. These defects were the despair of my mother. I fancy she had a weakness for my brother. At any rate, she spoiled him and forgave him his youthful sins, whereas she was very severe toward myself. To make up for it, my father overwhelmed me with kindness and indulgence. His tender love endeared him more and more to my heart; and so my good father is ever present to me, and I believe I have not forgotten a word he uttered in my hearing. How often, during 1789, did I think of something in sort prophetic which he said. He had come home from a philosophers' dinner where he had met Diderot, Helvetius and d'Alembert. He was so thoroughly dejected that my mother asked him what the matter was. "All I have heard to-night, my dear," he replied, "makes me believe that the world will soon be turned upside down."

I had spent one happy year at home when my father fell ill. After two months of suffering all hope of his recovery was abandoned. When he felt his last moments approaching, he declared a wish to see my brother and myself. We went close to his bedside, weeping bitterly. His face was terribly altered; his eyes and his features, usually so full of animation, were quite without expression, for the pallor and the chill of death were already upon him. We took his icy hand and covered it with kisses and tears. He made a last effort and sat up to give us his blessing. "Be happy, my children," was all he said. An hour later our poor father had ceased to live.

So heartbroken was I that it was long before I felt able to take to my crayons again. Doyen came to see us sometimes, and as he had been my father's best friend his visits were a great consolation. He it was who urged me to resume the occupation I loved, and in which, to speak truth, I found the only solace for my woe. It was then that I began to paint from nature. I accomplished several portraits—pastels and oils. I also drew from nature and from casts, often working by lamplight with Mlle. Boquet, with whom I was closely acquainted. I went to her house in the evenings; she lived in the Rue Saint Denis, where her father had a bric-à-brac shop. It was a long way off, since we lodged in the Rue de Cléry, opposite the Lubert mansion. My mother, therefore, insisted on my being escorted whenever I went. We likewise frequently repaired, Mlle. Boquet and I, to

Briard's, a painter, who lent us his etchings and his classical busts. Briard was but a moderate painter, although he did some ceilings of rather unusual conception. On the other hand, he could draw admirably, which was the reason why several young people went to him for lessons. His rooms were in the Louvre, and each of us brought her little dinner, carried in a basket by a nurse, in order that we might make a long day of it.

Mlle. Boquet was fifteen years old and I fourteen. We were rival beauties. I had changed completely and had become good looking. Her artistic abilities were considerable; as for mine, I made such speedy progress that I soon was talked about, and this resulted in my making the gratifying acquaintance of Joseph Vernet. That famous painter gave me cordial encouragement and much invaluable advice. I also got to know the Abbé Arnault, of the French Academy. He was a man of strong imaginative gifts, with a passion for literature and the arts. His conversation enriched me with ideas, if I may thus express myself. He would talk of music and painting with the most inspiring ardour. The Abbé was a warm partisan of Gluck, and at a later date brought the great composer to see me, for I, too, was passionately fond of music.

My mother was now proud of my face and figure; I was growing stouter, and presented the fresh appearance proper to youth. On Sundays she took me to the Tuileries. She was still handsome herself, and after the lapse of all these years I am free to confess that the manner in which we were so often followed by men embarrassed more than it flattered me. Seeing me so irremediably affected by our cruel loss, my mother deemed it best to take me out of myself by showing me pictures. Thus we went to the Luxembourg Palace, the gallery of which then contained some of Rubens's masterpieces, as well as numerous works by the greatest painters. At present nothing is to be seen there but pictures of the modern French school. I am the only painter of that class not represented. The old masters have since been removed to the Louvre. Rubens has lost much by the change: the difference between well or badly lighted pictures is the same as between well or badly played pieces of music.

We also saw some rich private collections, none of which, however, equalled that of the Palais Royal, made by the Regent and containing a conspicuous number of old Italian masters. As soon as I entered one of these galleries I at once became exactly like a bee, so much useful knowledge did I eagerly gather while intoxicated with bliss in the contemplation of the great masters. Besides, in order to improve myself, I copied some of the pictures of Rubens, some of Rembrandt's and Van Dyck's heads, as well as several heads of girls by Greuze, because these last were a good lesson to me in the demi-tints to be found in delicate flesh colouring. Van Dyck shows them also, but more finely. It is to these studies that I owe my improvement in the very important science of degradation of light on the salient parts of a head, so admirably done by Raphael, whose heads, it is true, combine all the perfections. But it is only in Rome, under the bright Italian sky, that Raphael can be properly judged. When, after years, I was enabled to see some of his masterpieces, which had never left their native home, I recognised Raphael to be above his high renown.

My father had left us penniless. But I was earning a deal of money, as I was already painting many portraits. This, however, was insufficient for household expenses, seeing that in addition I had to pay for my brother's schooling, his clothes, his books, and so on. My mother, therefore, saw herself obliged to remarry. She took a rich jeweller, whom we never had suspected of avarice, but who directly after the marriage·displayed his stinginess

by limiting us to the absolute necessities of life, although
I was good-natured enough to hand him over everything
I earned.   Joseph Vernet was greatly enraged; he coun-
selled me to grant an annuity and to keep the rest for
myself.   But I did not comply with this advice.   I was
afraid my mother might suffer in consequence, with such
a skinflint.   I detested the man, the more as he had
appropriated my father's wardrobe and wore all the
clothes just as they were, without having them altered
to fit him.

My young reputation attracted a number of strangers
to our house.   Several distinguished personages came to
see me, among them the notorious Count Orloff, one of
Peter the Third's assassins.   Count Orloff was a giant
in stature, and I remember his wearing a diamond of
enormous size in a ring.

About this time I painted a portrait of Count
Schouvaloff, Grand Chamberlain, then, I believe, about
sixty years old.   He combined amiability with perfect
manners, and, as he was an excellent man, was sought
after by the best company.

One of my visitors of eminence was Mme. Geoffrin, the
woman so famous for her brilliant social life.   Mme.
Geoffrin gathered at her house all the known men of
talent in literature and the arts, all foreigners of note
and the grandest gentlemen attached to the court.
Being neither of good family nor endowed with unusual
abilities, nor even possessing much money, she had
nevertheless made a position for herself in Paris unique
of its kind, and one that no woman could nowadays hope
to achieve.   Having heard me spoken of, she came to see
me one morning and said the most flattering things about
my person and my gifts.   Although she was not very
old, I should have put her down for a hundred, for not
only was she rather bent, but her dress gave her an aged
appearance.   She was clad in an iron-gray gown, and

on her head wore a large, winged cap, over which was a black shawl knotted under her chin. At present, on the other hand, women of her years succeed in making themselves look much younger by the care they bestow on their toilet.

Immediately after my mother's marriage we went to live at my stepfather's in the Rue Saint Honoré, opposite the terrace of the Palais Royal, which terrace our windows overlooked. I often saw the Duchess de Chartres walking in the garden with her ladies-in-waiting, and soon observed that she noticed me with kindly interest. I had recently finished a portrait of my mother which evoked a great deal of discussion at the time. The Duchess sent for me to come and paint her. She most obligingly commended my young talents to her friends, so that it was not long before I received a visit from the stately, handsome Countess de Brionne and her lovely daughter, the Princess de Lorraine, who were followed by all the great ladies of the court and the Faubourg Saint Germain.

Since I have acknowledged that I was stared at in the streets—the same is true of the theatres and other public places—and that I was the object of many attentions, it may readily be guessed that some admirers of my face gave me commissions to paint theirs. They hoped to get into my good graces in this way. But I was so absorbed in my art that nothing could take me away from it. Then, besides, the moral and religious principles my mother had instilled me with were a strong protection against the seductions surrounding me. Happily I never as yet had read a single novel. The first I read, "Clarissa Harlowe," was only after my marriage, and it interested me prodigiously. Before my marriage I read nothing but sacred literature, such as the moral precepts of the Holy Fathers, which contained everything one needs to know, and some of my brother's class-books.

To return to those gentlemen. As soon as I observed
any intention on their part of making sheep's eyes at me,
I would paint them looking in another direction than
mine, and then, at the least movement of the pupilla,
would say, "I am doing the eyes now." This vexed
them a little, of course, but my mother, who was always
present, and whom I had taken into my confidence, was
secretly amused.

On Sundays and saints' days, after hearing high mass,
my mother and my stepfather took me to the Palais
Royal for a walk. The gardens were then far more
spacious and beautiful than they are now, strangled and
straightened by the houses enclosing them. There was a
very broad and long avenue on the left arched by gigantic
trees, which formed a vault impenetrable to the rays of
the sun. There good society assembled in its best clothes.
The opera house was hard by the palace. In summer
the performance ended at half-past eight, and all
elegant people left even before it was over, in
order to ramble in the garden. It was the
fashion for the women to wear huge nosegays,
which, added to the perfumed powder sprinkled
in everybody's hair, really made the air one
breathed quite fragrant. Later, yet still before the
Revolution, I have known these assemblies to last until
two in the morning. There was music by moonlight,
out in the open; artists and amateurs sang songs; there
was playing on the harp and the guitar; the celebrated
Saint Georges often executed pieces on his violin. Crowds
flocked to the spot.

We never entered this avenue, Mlle. Boquet and I,
without attracting lively attention. We both were then
between sixteen and seventeen years old, Mlle. Boquet
being a great beauty. At nineteen she was taken with
the smallpox, which called forth such general interest
that numbers from all classes of society made anxious

inquiries, and a string of carriages was constantly drawn up outside her door.

She had a remarkable talent for painting, but she gave up the pursuit almost immediately after her marriage with M. Filleul, when the Queen made her Gatekeeper of the Castle of La Muette. Would that I could speak of the dear creature without calling her dreadful end to mind. Alas! how well I remember Mme. Filleul saying to me, on the eve of my departure from France, when I was to escape from the horrors I foresaw: "You are wrong to go. I intend to stay, because I believe in the happiness the Revolution is to bring us." And that Revolution took her to the scaffold! Before she quitted La Muette the Terror had begun. Mme. Chalgrin, a daughter of Joseph Vernet, and Mme. Filleul's bosom friend, came to the castle to celebrate her daughter's wedding—quietly, as a matter of course. However, the next day the Jacobins none the less proceeded to arrest Mme. Filleul and Mme. Chalgrin, who, they said, had wasted the candles of the nation. A few days later they were both guillotined.

Among the favourite walks were the Temple boulevards. Every day, though especially on Thursdays, hundreds of vehicles drove or stood in the roads where the cafés and shows still are. The young men on horseback caracoled about the carriages, as they did at Longchamps, for Longchamps was already in existence and even very brilliant. The side paths were full of immense throngs of pedestrians, enjoying the pastime of admiring or criticising all the lovely ladies, dressed in their best, who passed in fine carriages. At a certain spot, where the Café Turc now stands, a spectacle was to be seen which many a time made me burst into loud laughter. It was a long row of old women belonging to the Marais quarter, sitting gravely on chairs, their faces so thickly rouged that they looked precisely like dolls. As at that date the right to wear rouge was only conceded to women of high rank, these worthy ladies thought they must take advantage of the privilege to its full limit. One of our friends, who knew most of them, told us that their only employment at home was to play lotto from morning till night. He also said that one day, after he had returned from Versailles, some of them had asked him the news, that he had replied M. de La Perouse was to make a journey round the world, and that the hostess had thereupon exclaimed: "Gracious! What a lot of time the man must have on his hands!"

Years later, long after my marriage, I saw various little shows on this very boulevard. At one only did I attend often; that was Carlo Perico's "Fantoccini," which amused me vastly. These marionettes were so cleverly made, and their gestures were so natural, that the delusion sometimes succeeded. My little girl, six years old almost, did not at first suspect that the figures were not alive. I informed her as to the truth, and when, soon after, I took her to the Comédie Française, where my box was rather far from the stage, she asked me, "And those, mamma, are they alive?"

The Coliseum was another highly fashionable resort. It was established in one of the large squares of the Champs Elysées, in the form of a vast rotunda. In the middle was a lake of clear water, on which boatmen's races were held. You strolled round about in broad, gravelled avenues lined with benches. At nightfall every one left the garden to meet in a great hall where a full orchestra dispensed excellent music. At this period there also was on the Temple boulevard a place called the Summer Vauxhall, whose garden was simply a big space for walking in, bordered by covered tiers of seats for the convenience of good society. People gathered there before dark in warm weather, and the diversions of the day closed with a grand display of fireworks.

All these places were frequented much more than Tivoli is to-day. It is surprising, too, that the Parisians, who have nothing but the Tuileries and the Luxembourg, should have renounced those other resorts, which were half urban and half rural, where you went in the evening to get a breath of air and eat ices.

CHAPTER II

Up the Ladder of Fame

TEDIOUS SOJOURN IN THE COUNTRY — SOCIAL AMENITIES
IN PARIS — MLLE. VIGÉE BECOMES MME. LEBRUN —
PROGNOSTICATIONS OF UNHAPPY WEDLOCK — ON THE
LADDER OF FAME — SINGULARITIES OF ORIENTAL TASTE
— MARIE ANTOINETTE AS A MODEL — PAINTING THE
ROYAL FAMILY — HOW LOUIS XVIII. SANG—THE PRIN-
CESS DE LAMBALLE.

My detestable stepfather, annoyed no doubt by the
public admiration shown my mother, forbade us to go for
any more walks, and informed us that he was about to
take a place in the country. At this announcement
my heart beat with joy, for I was passionately fond of the
country. I had been sleeping near the foot of my mother's
bedstead, in a dark corner where the light of day never
penetrated. Every morning, whatever the weather might
be, my first care was to open the window wide, such was
my thirst for fresh air.

So my stepfather took a small cottage at Chaillot, and
we went there on Saturday, spent Sunday there, and
returned to Paris on Monday morning. Good heavens,
what a country! Imagine a tiny vicarage garden, without a tree, without any shelter from the blazing sun but
a little arbour, where my stepfather had planted some
beans and nasturtium, which refused to grow. At that
we only occupied a quarter of this delightful garden, for
it was divided into four by slender railings, and the three

16

other sections were let out to shopboys, who came every Sunday and amused themselves by shooting at the birds. The incessant noise threw me into a desperate state of mind, besides which I was terribly afraid of being killed by these marksmen, so inaccurate was their aim. I could not understand why this stupid, ugly place, the very recollection of which makes me yawn as I write, was "the country." At last my good angel brought to my rescue a friend of my mother's, who one day came to dine with us at Chaillot with her husband. Both were sorry for me in my exile, and sometimes took me out for a charming drive.

We went to Marly-le-Roi, and there I found a more beautiful spot than any I had seen in my life. On each side of the magnificent palace were six summer-houses communicating with one another by walks embowered with jessamine and honeysuckle. Water fell in cascades from the top of a hill behind the castle, and formed a large channel on which a number of swans floated. The handsome trees, the carpets of green, the flowers, the fountains, one of which spouted up so high that it was lost from sight—it was all grand, all regal; it all spoke of Louis XIV. One morning I met Queen Marie Antoinette walking in the park with several of the ladies of her court. They were all in white dresses, and so young and pretty that for a moment I thought I was in a dream. I was with my mother, and was turning away when the Queen was kind enough to stop me, and invited me to continue in any direction I might prefer. Alas! when I returned to France in 1802 I hastened to see my noble, smiling Marly. The palace, the trees, the cascades, and the fountains had all disappeared; scarcely a stone was left.

I found it very hard to quit those lovely gardens and go back to our hideous Chaillot. But we at last went back to Paris, and settled there for the winter. The time left over from my work I now spent in a most agreeable manner. From the age of fifteen I had been going out into the best society; and I knew all the celebrated artists, so that I received invitations from all sides. I very well remember the first time I dined in town with the sculptor Le Moine, who was then enjoying a great reputation. It was there I met the famous actor Lekain, who struck terror into my heart because of his wild and sinister appearance; his huge eyebrows only added to the fierce expression of his face. He scarcely talked at all, and ate enormously. At Le Moine's I made the acquaintance of Gerbier, the noted advocate, and of his daughter Mme. de Roissy, who was very beautiful, and one of the first women I made a portrait of. Grétry and Latour, an eminent pastellist, often came to these dinners at Le Moine's, which were highly convivial and amusing. It was then the custom to sing at dessert. When the turn of the young ladies came—to whom, I must admit, this custom was torture—they would turn pale and tremble all over, and consequently often sing very much out of tune. In spite of these dissonances, the dinners ended pleasantly, and we always rose from the table with regret, although we did not immediately order our carriages, as the fashion is to-day.

I cannot, however, speak of the dinners of the present day excepting through hearsay, in view of the fact that soon after the time I have just mentioned I stopped dining in town for good. A slight adventure I had made me determine to go out only in the evening. I had accepted an invitation to dine with Princess Rohan-Rochefort. All dressed and ready to get into my carriage, I was seized with a sudden desire to take a look at a portrait that I had begun that same morning. I had on a white satin dress, which I was wearing for the first time. I sat down on my chair opposite my easel without noticing that my palette was lying on the chair. It may readily be conceived that the state of my gown was such as to compel me to remain at home, and I resolved thenceforth to accept no invitations excepting to supper.

The dinners of Princess Rohan-Rochefort were delightful. The nucleus of the society was composed of the handsome Countess de Brionne and her daughter the Princess Lorraine, the Duke de Choiseul, the Cardinal de Rohan, and M. de Rulhières, the author of the "Disputes"; but the most agreeable without question of all the guests was the Duke de Lauzun; no one could possibly have been cleverer or more entertaining; we were all fascinated by him. The evening was usually filled up with playing and singing, and I often sang to my own accompaniment on the guitar. Supper was at half-past ten; we were never more than ten or twelve at table. We all vied with one another in sociability and wit. As for me, I was only a humble listener, and, although too young to appreciate the qualities of this conversation to the full, it spoiled me for ordinary conversation.

My life as a young girl was very unusual. Not only did my talent—feeble as it seemed to me when I thought of the great masters—cause me to be sought after and welcomed by society, but I sometimes was the object of attentions which I might call public, and of which, I avow, I was very proud. For example, I had made portraits of Cardinal Fleury and La Bruyère, copied from engravings of ancient date. I made a gift of them to the French Academy, which sent me a very flattering letter through the permanent secretary, d'Alembert. My presentation of these two portraits to the Academy also secured me the honour of a visit from d'Alembert, a dried up morsel of a man of exquisitely polished manners. He stayed a long time and looked my study all over, while he paid me a thousand compliments. After he had gone, a fine lady, who happened to be visiting me at the same time, asked me whether I had painted La Bruyère and Fleury from life. "I am a little too young for that," I answered, unable to refrain from a laugh, but very glad for the sake of the lady that the Academician had left before she put her funny question.

My stepfather having retired from business, we took up residence at the Lubert mansion, in the Rue de Cléry. M. Lebrun had just bought the house and lived there himself, and as soon as we were settled in it I began to examine the splendid masterpieces of all schools with which his lodgings were filled. I was enchanted at an opportunity of first-hand acquaintance with these works by great masters. M. Lebrun was so obliging as to lend me, for purposes of copying, some of his handsomest and most valuable paintings. Thus I owed him the best lessons I could conceivably have obtained, when, after a lapse of six months, he asked my hand in marriage. I was far from wishing to become his wife, though he was very well built and had a pleasant face. I was then twenty years old, and was living without anxiety as to the future, since I was already earning a deal of money, so that I felt no manner of inclination for matrimony. But my mother, who believed M. Lebrun to be very rich, incessantly plied me with arguments in favour of accepting such an advantageous match. At last I decided in the affirmative, urged especially by the desire to escape from the torture of living with my stepfather, whose bad temper had increased day by day since he had relinquished active pursuits. So little, however, did I feel inclined to sacrifice my liberty that, even on my way to church, I kept saying to myself, "Shall I say yes, or shall I say no?" Alas! I said yes, and in so doing exchanged present troubles for others. Not that M. Lebrun was a cruel man: his character exhibited a mixture of gentleness and liveliness; he was extremely obliging to everybody, and, in a word, quite an agreeable person. But his furious passion for gambling was at the bottom of the ruin of his fortune and my own, of which he had the entire disposal, so that in 1789, when I quitted France, I had not an income of twenty francs, although I had earned more than a million. He had squandered it all.

My marriage was kept secret for some time. M. Lebrun, who was supposed to marry the daughter of a Dutchman with whom he did a great business in pictures, asked me to make no announcement until he had wound up his affairs. To this I consented the more willingly that I did not give up my maiden name without regret, particularly as I was so well known by that name. But the keeping of the secret, which did not last long, was nevertheless fraught with disastrous consequences for my future. A number of people who simply believed that I was merely considering a match with M. Lebrun came to advise me to commit no such piece of folly. Auber, the crown jeweller, said to me in a friendly spirit: "It would be better for you to tie a stone to your neck and jump into the river than to marry Lebrun." Another day the Duchess d'Aremberg, accompanied by Mme. de Canillas, and Mme. de Souza, the Portuguese Ambassadress, all very young and pretty, came to offer their belated counsels a fortnight after the knot had been tied. "For heaven's sake," exclaimed the Countess, "on no account marry M. Lebrun! You will be miserable if you do!" And then she told me a lot of things which I was happy enough to disbelieve, but which only proved too true afterward. The announcement of my marriage put an end to these sad warnings, which, thanks to my dear painting, had little effect on my usual good spirits. I could not meet the orders for portraits that were showered upon me from every side. M. Lebrun soon got into the habit of pocketing my fees. He also hit upon the idea of making me give lessons in order to increase our revenues. I acceded to his wishes without a moment's thought.

The number of portraits I painted at this time was really prodigious. As I detested the female style of dress then in fashion, I bent all my efforts upon rendering it a little more picturesque, and was delighted when, after getting the confidence of my models, I was able to drape them according to my fancy. Shawls were not yet worn, but I made an arrangement with broad scarfs lightly intertwined round the body and on the arms, which was an attempt to imitate the beautiful drapings of Raphael and Domenichino. The picture of my daughter playing the guitar is an example. Besides, I could not endure powder. I persuaded the handsome Duchess de Grammont-Caderousse to put none on for her sittings. Her hair was ebony black, and I divided it on the forehead, disposing it in irregular curls. After the sitting, which ended at the dinner hour, the Duchess would not change her head-dress, but go to the theatre as she was. A woman of such good looks would, of course, set a fashion: indeed, this mode of doing the hair soon found imitators, and then gradually became general. This reminds me that in 1786, when I was painting the Queen, I begged her to use no powder, and to part her hair on the forehead. "I should be the last to follow that fashion," said the Queen, laughing; "I do not want people to say that I adopted it to hide my large forehead."

As I said, I was overwhelmed with orders and was very much in vogue. Soon after my marriage I was present at a meeting of the French Academy at which La Harpe read his discourse on the talents of women. When he arrived at certain lines of exaggerated praise, which I was hearing for the first time, and in which he extolled my art and likened my smile to that of Venus, the author of "Warwick" threw a glance at me. At once the whole assembly, without excepting the Duchess de Chartres and the King of Sweden—who both were witnessing the ceremonies—rose up, turned in my direction, and applauded with such enthusiasm that I almost fainted from confusion.

But these pleasures of gratified vanity were far from comparable with the joy I experienced in looking forward to motherhood. I will not attempt to describe the transports I felt when I heard the first cry of my child. Every mother knows what those feelings are.

Not long before that event I painted the Duchess de Mazarin, who was no longer young, but whose beauty had not yet faded. This Duchess de Mazarin was said to have been endowed on her birth by three fairies, Wealth, Duty and Ill-luck. Certain it is that the poor woman could undertake nothing, not even so much as entertaining a party of friends, without some mishap befalling. A number of tales of all sorts of untoward happenings were current. Here is one of the least known: One evening, having sixty people to supper, she conceived the plan of putting on the table an enormous pie, in which were imprisoned a hundred tiny living birds. At a sign from the Duchess the pie was opened, and the whole fluttering flock beat their wings against the faces of the guests and took refuge in the hair of the women, making nests of their elaborately built-up head-dresses. It may be imagined what consternation and excitement there was! It was impossible to get rid of the unfortunate birds, and at last the company was obliged to leave the table, while they blessed such a silly trick.

The Duchess de Mazarin was very stout; it took hours to lace her. One day, while she was being laced, a visitor was announced. One of her maids ran to the door and exclaimed: "You can't come in until we have arranged her meat." I remember that this excessive corpulency evoked the admiration of the Turkish Ambassadors. When asked at the opera to point out the woman that pleased them most of all the occupants of the boxes, they pointed without hesitation to the Duchess de Mazarın—because she was the fattest.

While speaking of ambassadors, I must not forget to say how I once painted two diplomats, who, though they were copper-coloured, nevertheless had splendid heads. In 1788 some envoys were sent to Paris by the Emperor Tippoo Sahib. I saw these Indians at the opera and they appeared to me so remarkably picturesque that I thought I should like to paint them. But as they communicated to their interpreter that they would never allow themselves to be painted unless the request came from the King, I managed to secure that favour from His Majesty. I repaired to the hotel where the strangers were lodging, for they wanted to be painted at home. On my arrival one of them brought in a jar of rose-water, with which he sprinkled my hands; then the tallest, whose name was Davich Kahn, gave me a sitting. I did him standing, with his hand on his dagger. He threw himself into such an easy, natural position of his own accord that I did not make him change it. I let the paint dry in another room, and began on the portrait of the old ambassador, whom I represented seated with his son next to him. The father especially had a magnificent head. Both were clad in flowing robes of white muslin worked with golden flowers, and these robes, a sort of long tunic with wide, up-turned sleeves, were held in place by gorgeous belts.

Mme. de Bonneuil, to whom I had spoken of my artistic sittings, very much wanted to see these ambassadors. They invited us both to dinner, and we accepted from sheer curiosity. Upon entering the dining-room we were rather surprised to see that the dinner was served on the floor, which obliged us to assume an attitude that was very much like lying down, following the example of our Oriental hosts. They helped us with their hands to the contents of the dishes. In one of these was a fricassee of sheep's feet with white sauce, highly spiced, and in another

some indescribable hash. Our meal was not exactly
pleasant; it was rather too much of a shock to us to see
those brown hands used as spoons. The ambassadors
had brought a young man with them who spoke a little
French. During my sittings Mme. de Bonneuil taught
him to sing a popular ditty. When we went to make our
farewells the young man recited his song, and expressed
his regret in parting from us by adding: "Ah! my
heart! how it weepeth!" which I found very Oriental
and very well put.

When Davich Kahn's portrait was dry I sent for it,
but he had hidden it behind his bed and would not give
it up, asserting that the picture still needed a soul. I could
only obtain my painting by employing strategy. When
the ambassador could not find it he put the responsibility
on his valet, and threatened to kill him. The interpreter
had all the trouble in the world to explain that it was not
the custom to kill one's valet in Paris, and informed
him, moreover, that the King of France had asked for
the portrait.

It was in the year 1779 that I painted the Queen for
the first time; she was then in the heyday of her youth
and beauty. Marie Antoinette was tall and admirably
built, being somewhat stout, but not excessively so. Her
arms were superb, her hands small and perfectly formed,
and her feet charming. She had the best walk of any
woman in France, carrying her head erect with a dignity
that stamped her queen in the midst of her whole court,
her majestic mien, however, not in the least diminishing
the sweetness and amiability of her face. To any one
who has not seen the Queen it is difficult to get an idea of
all the graces and all the nobility combined in her person.
Her features were not regular; she had inherited that long
and narrow oval peculiar to the Austrian nation. Her
eyes were not large; in colour they were almost blue, and
they were at the same time merry and kind. Her nose

was slender and pretty, and her mouth not too large, though her lips were rather thick.   But the most remarkable thing about her face was the splendour of her complexion.   I never have seen one so brilliant, and brilliant is the word, for her skin was so transparent that it bore no umber in the painting.   Neither could I render the real effect of it as I wished.   I had no colours to paint such freshness, such delicate tints, which were hers alone, and which I had never seen in any other woman.

At the first sitting the imposing air of the Queen at first frightened me greatly, but Her Majesty spoke to me so graciously that my fear was soon dissipated.   It was on that occasion that I began the picture representing her with a large basket, wearing a satin dress, and holding a rose in her hand.   This portrait was destined for her brother, Emperor Joseph II., and the Queen ordered two copies besides—one for the Empress of Russia, the other for her own apartments at Versailles or Fontainebleau.

I painted various pictures of the Queen at different times.   In one I did her to the knees, in a pale orange-red dress, standing before a table on which she was arranging some flowers in a vase.   It may be well imagined that I preferred to paint her in a plain gown and especially without a wide hoopskirt.   She usually gave these portraits to her friends or to foreign diplomatic envoys. One of them shows her with a straw hat on, and a white muslin dress, whose sleeves are turned up, though quite neatly.   When this work was exhibited at the Salon, malignant folk did not fail to make the remark that the Queen had been painted in her chemise, for we were then in 1786, and calumny was already busy concerning her.   Yet in spite of all this the portraits were very successful.

Toward the end of the exhibition a little piece was given at the Vaudeville Theatre, bearing the title, I think,

"The Assembling of the Arts." Brongniart, the architect, and his wife, whom the author had taken into his confidence, had taken a box on the first tier, and called for me on the day of the first performance. As I had no suspicion of the surprise in store for me, judge of my emotion when Painting appeared on the scene and I saw the actress representing that art copy me in the act of painting a portrait of the Queen. The same moment everybody in the parterre and the boxes turned toward me and applauded to bring the roof down. I can hardly believe that any one was ever more moved and more grateful than I was that evening.

I was so fortunate as to be on very pleasant terms with the Queen. When she heard that I had something of a voice we rarely had a sitting without singing some duets by Grétry together, for she was exceedingly fond of music, although she did not sing very true. As for her conversation, it would be difficult for me to convey all its charm, all its affability. I do not think that Queen Marie Antoinette ever missed an opportunity of saying something pleasant to those who had the honour of being presented to her, and the kindness she always bestowed upon me has ever been one of my sweetest memories.

One day I happened to miss the appointment she had given me for a sitting; I had suddenly become unwell. The next day I hastened to Versailles to offer my excuses. The Queen was not expecting me; she had had her horses harnessed to go out driving, and her carriage was the first thing I saw on entering the palace yard. I nevertheless went upstairs to speak with the chamberlains on duty. One of them, M. Campan, received me with a stiff and haughty manner, and bellowed at me in his stentorian voice, "It was yesterday, madame, that Her Majesty expected you, and I am very sure she is going out driving, and I am very sure she will give you no sitting to-day!" Upon my reply that I had simply come to

take Her Majesty's orders for another day, he went to
the Queen, who at once had me conducted to her room.
She was finishing her toilet, and was holding a book in
her hand, hearing her daughter repeat a lesson. My heart
was beating violently, for I knew that I was in the wrong.
But the Queen looked up at me and said most amiably,
"I was waiting for you all the morning yesterday; what
happened to you?"

"I am sorry to say, Your Majesty," I replied, "I was
so ill that I was unable to comply with Your Majesty's
commands. I am here to receive more now, and then
I will immediately retire."

"No, no! Do not go!" exclaimed the Queen. "I do
not want you to have made your journey for nothing!"
She revoked the order for her carriage and gave me a
sitting. I remember that, in my confusion and my
eagerness to make a fitting response to her kind words, I
opened my paint-box so excitedly that I spilled my brushes
on the floor. I stooped down to pick them up. "Never
mind, never mind," said the Queen, and, for aught I
could say, she insisted on gathering them all up herself.

When the Queen went for the last time to Fontainebleau, where the court, according to custom, was to appear
in full gala, I repaired there to enjoy that spectacle. I
saw the Queen in her grandest dress; she was covered with
diamonds, and as the brilliant sunshine fell upon her she
seemed to me nothing short of dazzling. Her head, erect
on her beautiful Greek neck, lent her as she walked such
an imposing, such a majestic air, that one seemed to see
a goddess in the midst of her nymphs. During the first
sitting I had with Her Majesty after this occasion I took
the liberty of mentioning the impression she had made
upon me, and of saying to the Queen how the carriage
of her head added to the nobility of her bearing. She
answered in a jesting tone, "If I were not Queen they
would say I looked insolent, would they not?"

The Queen neglected nothing to impart to her children the courteous and gracious manners which endeared her so to all her surroundings. I once saw her make her six-year-old daughter dine with a little peasant girl and attend to her wants. The Queen saw to it that the little visitor was served first, saying to her daughter, "You must do the honours."

The last sitting I had with Her Majesty was given me at Trianon, where I did her hair for the large picture in which she appeared with her children. After doing the Queen's hair, as well as separate studies of the Dauphin, Madame Royale, and the Duke de Normandie, I busied myself with my picture, to which I attached great importance, and I had it ready for the Salon of 1788. The frame, which had been taken there alone, was enough to evoke a thousand malicious remarks. "That's how the money goes," they said, and a number of other things which seemed to me the bitterest comments. At last I sent my picture, but I could not muster up the courage to follow it and find out what its fate was to be, so afraid was I that it would be badly received by the public. In fact, I became quite ill with fright. I shut myself in my room, and there I was, praying to the Lord for the success of my "Royal Family," when my brother and a host of friends burst in to tell me that my picture had met with universal acclaim. After the Salon, the King, having had the picture transferred to Versailles, M. d'Angevilliers, then minister of the fine arts and director of royal residences, presented me to His Majesty. Louis XVI. vouchsafed to talk to me at some length and to tell me that he was very much pleased. Then he added, still looking at my work, "I know nothing about painting, but you make me like it."

The picture was placed in one of the rooms at Versailles, and the Queen passed it going to mass and returning. After the death of the Dauphin, which occurred early in

the year 1789, the sight of this picture reminded her so
keenly of the cruel loss she had suffered that she could not
go through the room without shedding tears. She
then ordered M. d'Angevilliers to have the picture taken
away, but with her usual consideration she informed
me of the fact as well, apprising me of her motive for the
removal. It is really to the Queen's sensitiveness that
I owed the preservation of my picture, for the fishwives
who soon afterward came to Versailles for Their Majesties
would certainly have destroyed it, as they did the
Queen's bed, which was ruthlessly torn apart.

I never had the felicity of setting eyes on Marie Antoinette after the last court ball at Versailles. The ball was
given in the theatre, and the box where I was seated was
so situated that I could hear what the Queen said. I
observed that she was very excited, asking the young
men of the court to dance with her, such as M. Lameth,
whose family had been overwhelmed with kindness by
the Queen, and others, who all refused, so that many
of the dances had to be given up. The conduct of
these gentlemen seemed to me exceedingly improper;
somehow their refusal likened a sort of revolt—
the prelude to revolts of a more serious kind. The
Revolution was drawing near; it was, in fact, to burst
out before long.

With the exception of the Count d'Artois, whose portrait I never did, I successively painted the whole royal
family—the royal children; Monsieur, the King's brother,
afterward Louis XVIII.; Madame Royale; the Countess
d'Artois; Madame Elisabeth. The features of this last-
named Princess were not regular, but her face expressed
gentle affability, and the freshness of her complexion was
remarkable; altogether, she had the charm of a pretty
shepherdess. She was an angel of goodness. Many
a time have I been a witness to her deeds of charity on
behalf of the poor. All the virtues were in her heart:

she was indulgent, modest, compassionate, devoted. In the Revolution she displayed heroic courage; she was seen going forward to meet the cannibals who had come to murder the Queen, saying, "They will mistake me for her!"

The portrait I made of Monsieur favoured me with the occasion to become acquainted with a prince whose wit and learning one could extol without flattery; it was impossible not to find pleasure in the conversation of Louis XVIII., who talked on all subjects with equal degrees of taste and understanding. However, for the sake of variety no doubt, at some of our sittings he would sing to me, and he would sing such common songs that I was unable to understand how these trivial things had ever reached the court. He sang more out of tune than any one in the whole world. "How do you think I sing?" he asked me one day. "Like a prince, Your Highness," was my reply.

The Marquis de Montesquiou, equerry-in-chief to Monsieur, would send me a fine carriage and six to bring me to Versailles and take me back with my mother, who accompanied me at my request. All along the road people stood at the windows to see me pass, and every one took their hats off. This homage rendered to six horses and an outrider amused me, for on returning to Paris I got into a cab, and nobody took the slightest notice of me.

About this time I also painted the Princess de Lamballe. Without being actually pretty, she appeared so at a little distance; she had small features, complexion of dazzling freshness, superb blond locks, and was generally elegant in person. The unhappy end of this unfortunate Princess is sufficently well known, and so is the devotion to which she fell a victim. For in 1793, when she was at Turin, entirely out of harm's way, she returned to France upon learning that the Queen was in danger.

CHAPTER III

Work and Pleasure

IMPRESSIONS OF FLANDERS — THE AUTHORESS'S ELECTION
TO THE FRENCH ROYAL ACADEMY OF PAINTING — HER
DEVOTION TO WORK — SOCIAL PLEASURES — A TALE
OF AN ARTIST'S EXTRAVAGANCE — CALONNE AND CAL-
UMNY — M. LEBRUN ALLOWS HIS WIFE NOUGHT PER
CENT. OF HER EARNINGS — A DRAMATIC CONSTELLATION
— THE INCOMPARABLE MME. DUGAZON.

IN 1782 M. Lebrun took me to Flanders, whither he was
called by affairs of business. A sale was then being held
in Brussels of a splendid collection of pictures belonging
to Prince Charles, and we went to view it. I found
there several ladies of the court who met me with great
kindness, among them the Princess d'Aremberg, whom
I had frequently seen in Paris. But the acquaintance
upon which I congratulated myself most was that of the
Prince de Ligne, whom I had not known before, and
who has left an historic reputation for wit and hospitality.
He invited us to visit his gallery, where I admired various
masterpieces, especially portraits by Van Dyck and
heads by Rubens, for he owned but few Italian pictures.
He was also good enough to receive us at his magnificent
house at Bel-Oeil. I remember that he made us ascend
to an outlook, built on the top of a hill commanding the
whole of his estate and the whole of the country round
about. The perfect air we breathed up there, together
with the delightful view, was something enchanting.

What was best of all in this lovely place was the greetings of the master of the house, who for his graceful mind and manners never had an equal.

The town of Brussels seemed to me prosperous and lively. In high society, for instance, people were so wrapped up in pleasure-seeking that several friends of the Prince de Ligne sometimes left Brussels at noon, arriving at the opera in Paris just in time to see the curtain go up, and when the performance was over returned to Brussels, travelling all night. That is what I call being fond of the opera!

We quitted Brussels to go to Holland. I was very much pleased with Saardam and Maestricht; these two little towns are so clean and so very well kept that one envies the lot of the inhabitants. The streets being very narrow and provided with canals, one does not ride in carriages, but on horseback, and small boats are used for the transportation of merchandise. The houses, which are very low, have two doors—the birth door, and the death door, through which one only passes in a coffin. The roofs of these houses shine as if they were of burnished steel, and everything is so scrupulously clean that I remember seeing, outside a blacksmith's shop, a sort of lamp hanging up, which was gilded and polished as though intended for a lady's chamber. The women of the people in this part of Holland seemed to me very handsome, but were so timid that the sight of a stranger made them run away at once. I suppose, however, that the presence of the French in their country may have tamed them.

We finally visited Amsterdam, and there I saw in the town hall the magnificent painting by Van Loo representing the assembled aldermen. I do not believe that in the whole realm of painting there is anything finer, anything truer; it is nature itself. The aldermen are dressed in black; faces, hands, draping—all done inimitably.

These men are alive; you think you are with them. I
persuaded myself that this picture must be the most perfect of its kind; I could not tear myself away from it,
and the impression it made on me was strong enough
to make it ever present in my mind.

We returned to Flanders to see the masterpieces of
Rubens. They were hung much more advantageously
than they have been since in Paris, for they all produce
a wonderful effect in those Flemish churches. Other
works by the same master adorn some private galleries.
In one of them, at Antwerp, I found the famous "Straw
Hat," which has lately been sold to an Englishman for
a large sum. This admirable picture represents a woman
by Rubens. It delighted and inspired me to such a
degree that I made a portrait of myself at Brussels,
striving to obtain the same effects. I painted myself
with a straw hat on my head, a feather, and a garland of
wild flowers, holding my palette in my hand. And when
the portrait was exhibited at the Salon I feel free to confess that it added considerably to my reputation. The
celebrated Müller made an engraving after it, but it must
be understood that the dark shadows of an engraving
spoiled the whole effect of such a picture. Soon after my
return from Flanders, the portrait I had mentioned, and
several other works of mine, were the cause of Joseph
Vernet's decision to propose me as a member of the
Royal Academy of Painting. M. Pierre, then first
Painter to the King, made strong opposition, not wishing, he said, that women should be admitted, although
Mme. Vallayer-Coster, who painted flowers beautifully,
had already been admitted, and I think Mme. Vien had
been, too. M. Pierre, a very mediocre painter, was a
clever man. Besides, he was rich, and this enabled him
to entertain artists luxuriously. Artists were not so
well off in those days as they are now. His opposition
might have become fatal to me if all true picture-lovers

had not been associated with the Academy, and if they had not formed a cabal, in my favour, against M. Pierre's. At last I was admitted, and presented my picture "Peace Bringing Back Plenty."

I continued to paint furiously, sometimes taking three sittings in the course of a single day. After-dinner sittings, which fatigued me extremely, brought about a disorder of my stomach, so that I could digest nothing and became wretchedly thin. My friends made me consult a doctor, who ordered me to sleep every day after dinner. At first it was some trouble to me to follow this habit, but by remaining in my room with the blinds down I gradually succeeded. I am persuaded that I owe my life to this rule. All I regret about that enforced rest is that it deprived me for good and all of the amusement of dining in town, and as I devoted the whole morning to painting I never was able to see my friends until the evening. Then, it is true, none of the pleasures of society were closed to me, for I spent my evenings in the politest and most accomplished circles.

After my marriage I still lived in the Rue de Cléry, where M. Lebrun had large, richly furnished apartments and kept his pictures by all the great masters. As for myself, I was reduced to occupying a small anteroom, and a bedroom, which also served for my drawing-room. This was unpretentiously papered and furnished, and there I received my visitors from town and court. Every one was eager to come to my evening parties, which were sometimes so crowded that marshals of France sat on the floor for want of chairs. I remember that the Marshal de Noailles, who was very stout and very old, one evening had the greatest difficulty in getting up again.

I was fond of flattering myself, of course, that all these grand people came for my sake. But, as it always was in open houses, some came to see the others, and most of them to enjoy the best music to be heard in

Paris. Such famous composers as Grétry, Sacchini, and Martini often played pieces from their operas at my house before the first performance. Our usual singers were Garat, Asvedo, Richer, and Mme. Todi. My sister-in-law, who had a very fine voice and could sing anything at sight, was very useful to us. Sometimes I sang myself, but without much method, I confess. Garat may, perhaps, be mentioned as the most extraordinary virtuoso who ever lived. Not only did no difficulties exist for his flexible throat, but as to expression he had no rival, and I think that no one has ever sung Gluck as well as he. For instrumental music I had as a violinist Viotti, whose playing, so full of grace, of force and expression, was ravishing. I also had Jarnovick, Maestrino, and Prince Henry of Prussia, an excellent amateur, who brought this first violinist besides. Salentin played the hautboy, Hulmandel and Cramer the piano. Mme. de Montgerou came once, soon after her marriage. Although she was very young then, she nevertheless astonished my friends, who were very hard to please, by her admirable execution, and especially by her expression; she really made the instrument speak. Mme. Montgerou has since taken first rank as a pianist, and distinguished herself as a composer.

At the time I gave my concerts people had taste and leisure for amusement, and even some years later the love of music was so general that it occasioned a serious quarrel between those who were called Gluckists and Piccinists. All amateurs were divided into two opposing factions. The usual field of battle was the garden of the Palais Royal. There the partisans of Gluck and the partisans of Piccini went at each other with such violence that there was more than one duel to record. The women who were usually present comprised the Marquise de Grollier, Mme. de Verdun, the Marquise de Sabran, who afterward married the Chevalier de Boufflers,

Mme. le Couteux du Molay—my best friends, all four of them—the Marquise de Rougé, Mme. de Pezé, her friend, whom I painted in the same picture with her, and a host of other French ladies, whom, owing to the smallness of my rooms, I could receive but rarely, and all sorts of distinguished foreign ladies. As for men, the list would be too long to write it down.

From this crowd I selected the cleverest for invitation to my suppers, which the Abbé Delille, the poet Lebrun, the Chevalier de Boufflers, the Viscount de Ségur, and others contributed to make the most entertaining in Paris. He can form no opinion of what society once was in France who has not seen the time when, all of the day's business absolved, a dozen or fifteen delightful people met at the house of a hostess to finish their evening. The ease and the refined merriment which reigned at these light evening repasts gave them a charm which dinners can never have. A sort of confidence and intimacy prevailed among the guests; it was by such suppers that the good society of Paris showed its superiority to that of all Europe. At my house, for instance, we met at about nine o'clock. No one ever talked politics, but we chatted about literature and told anecdotes of the hour. Sometimes we diverted ourselves by acting charades, and sometimes the Abbé Delille or the poet Lebrun read us some of their compositions. At ten o'clock we sat down to table. My suppers were of the simplest. They always consisted of some fowl, a fish, a dish of vegetables, and a salad, so that if I succumbed to the temptation of keeping back some visitors there really was nothing more for any one to eat. But that mattered little; the hours passed like minutes, and at midnight the company broke up.

I not only gave suppers at my own house, but frequently supped in town. Sometimes there was dancing,

and there was no crowding to suffocation, as there is
nowadays. Eight persons only performed the square
dances, and the women who were not dancing could at
least look on, for the men stood behind them. I often
went to spend the evening at M. de Rivière's, in charge
of the Saxon legation, a man distinguished as much
by his wit as by his good qualities. We played comedies
there, and comic operas. His daughter (my sister-in-
law) sang excellently, and could pass for a good society
actress. M. de Rivière's eldest son was charming in
comic parts, and I was given the use of a few professionals
in opera and drama. Mme. Laruette, some years retired
from the stage, did not disdain our troupe. She played
with us in several operas, and her voice was still fresh
and fine. My brother Vigée played leading parts with
very great success. In short, all our actors were good—
excepting Talma. My saying this will no doubt make
my readers laugh. The fact is, that Talma, who acted
lovers' parts with us, was so awkward and diffident that
no one could then possibly have foreseen how great an
actor he would become. My surprise was therefore
very great when I saw our leading man surpass Larive
and take the place of Lekain. But the time it took
to operate this change, and all of the same kind, proves
to me that the dramatic talent takes longer to reach
perfection than any other.

One evening, when I had invited a dozen or more
friends to hear a recital by the poet Lebrun, and while
we were waiting for them, my brother read aloud to
me a few pages of "Anacharsis." Arriving at the place
where, in the description of a Greek dinner, the method
of preparing various sauces is explained, "We ought,"
said my brother, "to try this to-night." I at once
ordered up my cook and instructed her properly, deciding
that she was to make a certain sauce for the chicken
and another for the eel. As I was expecting some very

pretty women, I conceived the idea of Greek costumes, in order to give M. de Vaudreuil and M. Boutin a surprise, knowing they would not arrive until ten o'clock. My studio, full of things I used for draping my models, would furnish me with enough material for garments, and the Count de Parois, who lived in my house in the Rue de Cléry, owned a superb collection of Etruscan pottery. It happened that he came to see me that evening. I confided my project to him, so that he supplied me with a number of drinking-cups and vases, from among which I took my choice. I cleaned all these articles myself, and arranged them on a table of mahogany without a tablecloth. This done, I put behind the chairs a large screen, which I took the precaution of concealing under some hangings looped up at intervals, as may be seen in Poussin's pictures. A hanging lamp threw a strong light on the table. All was now prepared except my costumes, when Joseph Vernet's daughter, the charming Mme. Chalgrin, was first to arrive. I immediately took her in hand, doing her hair and dressing her up. Then came Mme. de Bonneuil, so remarkable for her beauty, and Mme. Vigée, my sister-in-law, who, without being pretty, had the most beautiful eyes imaginable. And there they were, all three, metamorphosed into veritable Athenians. Lebrun came in; we wiped off his powder, undid his side curls, and put a wreath of laurels on his head. Then the Marquis de Cubières arrived. While we sent for a guitar of his, which he had turned into a gilded lyre, I attended to his costume, and then likewise dressed up M. de Rivière, and Chaudet, the famous sculptor.

The hour was waxing late. I had little time to think of myself. But as I always wore white gowns in the form of a tunic—now called a blouse—it was sufficient to put a veil and a wreath of flowers on my head. I took particular pains in costuming my daughter, darling

child that she was, and Mlle. de Bonneuil, now Mme.
Regnault d'Angély, who was as lovely as an angel.
Both were ravishing to behold, bearing a very light
antique vase, in readiness to serve us with drink.

At half past nine the preparations were ended, and at
ten we heard the carriage of the Count de Vaudreuil
and of Boutin roll in, and when these two gentlemen
arrived before the door of the dining-room, whose two
leaves I had thrown open, they found us singing Gluck's
chorus, "The God of Paphos," with M. de Cubières
accompanying us on his lyre. Never in all my days
have I seen two such astonished faces as those of M. de
Vaudreuil and his companion. They were so surprised
and delighted that they stood motionless for a long
time before they could make up their minds to take the
seats we had reserved for them.

Besides the two courses I have mentioned, we had for
supper a cake made with honey and Corinth raisins, and
two dishes of vegetables. I confess that that evening
we drank a bottle of old Cyprus wine, which had been
presented to me. But that was the whole of our dissi-
pation. We nevertheless remained a long time at table,
where Lebrun recited to us several odes of "Anacreon,"
which he had translated, and I think I never spent a
more amusing evening. M. Boutin and M. de Vaudreuil
were so enthusiastic that the next day they told all their
friends about the entertainment.

Some of the women of the court asked me to repeat
the performance. I declined for various reasons, and
some of them felt hurt by my refusal. Soon the report
spread in society that this supper had cost me twenty
thousand francs. The King spoke of it with annoyance
to the Marquis de Cubières, who fortunately had been
one of my guests, and who therefore was able to convince
His Majesty how foolish the accusation was. Nevertheless, what was estimated at Versailles at the modest

price of twenty thousand francs was increased at Rome to forty thousand. At Vienna the Baroness de Strogonoff informed me that I had spent sixty thousand francs on my Greek supper. At St. Petersburg the sum fixed upon was eighty thousand francs. In reality, the supper had occasioned an outlay of nearly fifteen francs!

Although, as I am sure, I was the most harmless creature who ever drew breath, I had enemies. A few years before the Revolution I did the portrait of M. de Calonne, which I exhibited at the Salon of 1785. I painted that minister in a sitting position and as far as the knees, which caused Mlle. Arnould to say, when she looked at it: "Mme. Lebrun cut off his legs, so that he should not get away." Unfortunately, this little witticism was not the only one my picture evoked; I was made the butt of calumnies of the most odious description. There were a thousand stories circulated as to the payment of the portrait, some asserting that the minister had given me a quantity of sweetmeats wrapped in bank-notes, others that I had received in a pasty a sum large enough to ruin the treasury. The fact is, that M. de Calonne had sent me four thousand francs in a box worth twenty louis. Some of the people who were with me when the box arrived can certify this. They were even surprised at the smallness of the amount, for not long before, M. de Beaujon, whom I had painted in the same style, had sent me eight thousand francs, without any one considering this fee too large.

I cared so little about money that I scarcely knew the value of it. The Countess de la Guiche, who is still alive, can affirm that, upon coming to me to have her portrait painted and telling me that she could afford no more than a thousand francs, I answered that M. Lebrun wished me to do none for less than two thousand. My closest friends all know that M. Lebrun took all the money I earned, on the plea of investing it in his business.

I often had no more than six francs in my pocket and
in the world.   When in 1788 I painted the picture of
the handsome Prince Lubomirskia, who was then grown
up, his aunt, the Princess Lubomirska, remitted twelve
thousand francs to me, out of which I begged M. Lebrun
to let me keep forty; but he would not let me have even
that, alleging that he needed the whole sum to liquidate
a promissory note.

My indifference to money no doubt proceeded from the
fact that wealth was not necessary to me.   Since that
which made my house pleasant required no extravagance,
I always lived very economically.   I spent very little
on dress; I was even reproached for neglecting it, for
I wore none but white dresses of muslin or lawn, and
never wore elaborate gowns excepting for my sittings
at Versailles.   My head-dress cost me nothing, because
I did my hair myself, and most of the time I wore a
muslin cap on my head, as may be seen from my portraits.

One of my favourite distractions was going to the play,
and I can vow that so many talented actors were on the
Paris stage that many of them have had no successors.
I remember perfectly having seen the renowned
Lekain act, whose ugliness, monstrous as it was, was
not apparent in all his parts.   But when he played the
rôle of Orosmane, in which I once saw him, I was very
near the stage, and his turban made him so hideous
that, although I admired his fine bearing, he frightened
me.   Mlle. Dumesnil, although she was short and very
ugly, sent her audiences into transports in her great
tragic rôles.   It sometimes happened that Mlle. Dumesnil
acted through a portion of the play without producing
any impression; then, all of a sudden, she would change;
her gestures, her voice and her features all became so
intensely tragic that she brought down the house.
I was assured that before coming on the stage she was
in the habit of drinking a bottle of wine, and that another

was held in reserve for her in the wings. The most
brilliant first appearance I can remember was Mlle.
Raucourt's in the part of Dido, when she was eighteen
or twenty at the most. The beauty of her face, her
figure, her voice, her declamation—everything fore-
shadowed a perfect actress. To so many advantages
she added an air of remarkable decency and a reputation
of severe morals, which caused her to be sought after
by our greatest ladies. She was presented with jewelry,
with theatrical costumes, and with money for herself
and her father, who was always with her. Later on
she changed her habits very much.

Talma, our last great tragic actor, in my opinion surpassed all the others. There was genius in his acting.
It may also be said that he revolutionised the art, in the
first place through banishing the bombastic and affected
style of delivery by his natural, sincere elocution, and
secondly through bringing about an innovation in dress,
attiring himself like a Greek or a Roman when he played
Achilles or Brutus—for which I was heartily grateful to
him. Talma had one of the finest heads and one of the
most mobile countenances imaginable, and, however
impetuous his acting became, always kept dignified, which
seems to me a prime quality in a tragic actor. He was
a very good man, and the best tempered individual in
the world. It was his custom to make no fuss in society;
in order to make him respond, it needed something in
the conversation which would stir one of his deepest
interests, and then he was well worth listening to, particularly when he talked about his art. Comedy was perhaps
better off still for talent than tragedy. I often had the
good fortune to see Préville on the stage. There, indeed,
was the perfect, the inimitable artist! His acting, so
clever, so natural, and so full of fun, was at the same
time most varied. He would play in turn Crispin,
Sosie, and Figaro, and you would not know it was the

same man, so inexhaustible were his comic resources.
Dugazon, his successor in humorous parts, would have
been an excellent comedian if a desire to make the public
laugh had not often led him into being farcical. He
played certain parts of valets admirably. Dugazon
behaved villainously in the Revolution: he was one of
those who went for the King to Varennes, and an eye-
witness told me that he had seen him at the carriage door
with a gun on his shoulder. Be it observed that this man
had been overwhelmed with favours by the court, and
especially by the Count d'Artois.

I also witnessed Mlle. Contat's first appearance. She
was extremely pretty and well made, but did her work so
badly at first that no one foresaw what a fine actress she
was to become. Her charming face was not sufficient
to protect her from hisses when she played the part
confided to her by Beaumarchais, of Susanna in "The
Marriage of Figaro." But from that moment on she
advanced further and further on the path of success.

At a period when all of the great actors were beginning
to age, a young talent arose that to-day is the ornament
of the French stage: Mlle. Mars was then playing the
parts of young girls in the most highly accomplished
manner; she excelled in that of Victorine in "The
Unwitting Philosopher," and in a dozen others in
which she never had an equal. For it was impossible
for any one else to be so true to life and so affecting; it
was nature at its best. Fortunately, that face, that
figure, that bewitching voice are so perfectly preserved
that Mlle. Mars has no age, nor, I believe, ever will have,
and the public proves every night by its applause that it
shares my opinion.

I remember having seen Sophie Arnould twice at the
opera, in "Castor and Pollux." I recollect that she seemed
to me to possess grace and feeling. As for her abilities
as a singer, the music of that epoch disgusted me so that

I did not listen to it enough to be able to speak about it now. Mlle. Arnould was not pretty; her mouth spoiled her face; only her eyes conveyed the cleverness which made her famous. A great number of her witty sayings have been passed round from mouth to mouth or printed.

A woman whose superior gifts delighted us for a long time was Mlle. Arnould's successor. This was Mme. Saint Huberti, whom one must have heard in order to understand how far lyric tragedy can go. Mme. Saint Huberti had not only a superb voice, but was also a great actress. Her good fate ordained that she should sing the operas of Piccini, Sacchini and Gluck, and all this music, so beautiful, so expressive, exactly suited her talent, which was full of significance, of sincerity and of nobility. She was not good-looking, but her face was entrancing because of its soulfulness. The Count d'Entraigues, a very fine, handsome man, and very distinguished through his intellect, fell in love with her and married her. When the Revolution broke out they escaped to London together. It was there that one evening they were both murdered, without either the murderers or their motives ever being discovered.

In the ballet, likewise noted for people with great capabilities, Gardel and Vestris the elder were first. Vestris was tall and imposing, and was not to be excelled in dances of the grave and sedate order. I could not prescribe the grace with which he took off and put back his hat at the bow preceding the minuet. All the young women of the court took lessons from him, before their presentation, in making the three courtesies. Vestris the elder was succeeded by his son, the most astonishing dancer to be seen, such were his combined gracefulness and lightness. Although our dancers of the present day by no means spare us their pirouettes, certainly no one could ever do as many as he did. He would suddenly rise toward the sky in such a marvellous manner that one thought he must have wings, and this made old Vestris say, "If my son touches the ground it is only from politeness to his colleagues."

Mlle. Guimard had another sort of talent altogether. Her dancing was only a sketch; she did nothing but take short steps, but executed them with such fascinating motions that the public awarded her the palm over all other female dancers. She was short, slight, very well shaped, and, although plain, her features were such that at the age of forty-five she looked no more than fifteen when on the stage.

I now come to one whose entire dramatic career I have been able to follow—the best talent the Opéra-Comique had to show, Mme. Dugazon. Never has such reality been seen upon the stage. The actress disappeared, and gave place to the actual Babet, Countess d'Albert, or Nicolette. Her voice was rather weak, but it was strong enough for laughter, for tears, for all situations, for all parts. Grétry and Delayrac, who wrote for her, were mad about her. No one ever again played Nina like her— Nina, so decent and so passionate at once, and so unhappy and so touching that the mere sight of her made the audience shed tears. Mme. Dugazon was a royalist, heart and soul. Of this she gave the public a proof, when the Revolution was well advanced, in playing the part of the maid in "Unforeseen Events." The Queen was witnessing the performance, and in a duet begun by the valet, with "I love my master dearly," Mme. Dugazon, whose answer was "Ah, how I love my mistress!" turned toward the Queen's box, laid her hand over her heart, and sang her reply in a melting voice while she bowed to Her Majesty. I was told that the public—and such a public—afterward sought revenge by attempting to make her sing some horrible thing which had come into vogue and was often heard in the theatres. But Mme. Dugazon would not yield. She left the stage.

CHAPTER IV

EXILE

A GALLIC MAECENAS — ANECDOTE CONCERNING BEAU-
MARCHAIS — THE DUKE DE NIVERNAIS — MME. DU
BARRY SKETCHED IN WORDS — AND PAINTED IN OILS
— RUMBLINGS OF THE REVOLUTION — MME. LEBRUN'S
FEARSOME JOURNEY TO ITALY — RENEWED ARTISTIC
ACTIVITY AT ROME — EASTER SUNDAY AT ST. PETER'S
— FASCINATION OF THE ETERNAL CITY — VANITIES
AND VIOLENCES OF ITS PEOPLE.

THE same year that I went to Flanders I made a stay of
some length at Raincy. The Duke d'Orléans, the father
of Philippe Egalité, who was then living there, sent for
me to paint his portrait and Mme. de Montesson's. I
cannot recall a certain incident without laughing, though
it annoyed me considerably at the time. During Mme.
de Montesson's sittings the old Princess de Conti came
to see her one day, and this Princess persisted in addressing me as "Miss." It is true that it had formerly been the
custom for great ladies to behave in this way toward
their inferiors, but that sort of court snobbery had gone
out with Louis XV.

Another noted country estate, Gennevilliers, belonged
to the Count de Vaudreuil, one of the most amiable of
men. The Count de Vaudreuil had bought this property
largely for His Highness the Count d'Artois, because it
included fine hunting-grounds. The purchaser had done
much to embellish the place. The house was furnished
in the best taste, and without ostentation; there was a

47

small but charming theatre in the house, where my sister-in-law, my brother, M. de Riviére and I often played in comic operas with Mme. Dugazon, and Garat, Cailleau, and Laruette. The Count d'Artois and his company witnessed our performances. The last given in the theatre at Gennevilliers was "The Marriage of Figaro" by the actors of the Comédie-Française. Mlle. Contat was delightful in the part of Suzanne. Dialogue, couplets, and all the rest were aimed against the court, of which a large part was present. This extravagance benefited no one, but Beaumarchais was none the less intoxicated with joy. As there were complaints of the heat, he allowed no time for the windows to be opened, but smashed all the panes with his walking-stick.

The Count de Vaudreuil came to repent of having given his patronage to the "Marriage of Figaro." In fact, very soon after the performance mentioned Beaumarchais asked for an audience. This being at once granted, he arrived at Versailles at such an early hour that the Count had only just got up. The dramatist then broached a financial project which he had hatched out, and which was to bring in a vast fortune. He concluded by proposing to hand over to M. de Vaudreuil a large sum if he would engage to carry the affair through successfully. The Count listened quite calmly, and when Beaumarchais finished speaking, answered: "M. de Beaumarchais, you could not come at a more favourable time, for I have spent a good night, my digestion is in good order, and I never felt better than I do to-day. If you had made such a proposition to me yesterday I would have thrown you out of the window."

Another fine country place I visited was Villette. The Marquise de Villette, nicknamed Lovely and Lovable, having invited me, I went to pass a few days there. On one occasion we found a man painting fences in the park. This painter was working with such expedition that M.

de Villette complimented him upon it. "Oh!" was the reply, "I'd undertake to cover up in a day all that Rubens painted in his whole life!"

I dined several times at Saint Ouen, with the Duke de Nivernais, who owned a very handsome residence there, and who gathered about him the most agreeable company it was possible to meet. The Duke, always praised for his elegant and pointed wit, had manners that were dignified and gentle and without the slightest affectation. He was particularly distinguished for his extreme civility to women of all ages. In this respect I might speak of him as a model of whom I would never have found a copy if I had not known the Count de Vaudreuil, who, much younger than the Duke de Nivernais, added to his refined gallantry a politeness that was the more flattering since it came from the heart. In fact, it is very difficult to convey an idea to-day of the urbanity, the graceful ease, in a word the affability of manner which made the charm of Parisian society forty years ago. The women reigned then; the Revolution dethroned them. The Duke de Nivernais was very small and very lean. Although very old when I knew him, he was still full of life; he was passionately fond of poetry, and wrote charming verses.

I also dined frequently at the Marshal de Noailles's, in his fine mansion situated at the entrance to Saint Germain. There was then an immense park there, admirably kept. The Marshal was highly sociable; his cleverness and good spirits infected all his guests, whom he selected from among the literary celebrities and the most distinguished people of the town and the court.

It was in 1786 that I went for the first time to Louveciennes, where I had promised to paint Mme. Du Barry. She might then have been about forty-five years old. She was tall without being too much so; she had a certain roundness, her throat being rather pronounced

but very beautiful; her face was still attractive, her
features were regular and graceful; her hair was
ashy, and curly like a child's. But her complexion
was beginning to fade. She received me with much
courtesy, and seemed to me very well behaved, but
I found her more spontaneous in mind than in
manner: her glance was that of a coquette, for her
long eyes were never quite open, and her pronunciation
had something childish which no longer suited her
age.

She lodged me in a part of the building where I was
greatly put out by the continual noise. Under my
room was a gallery, sadly neglected, in which busts,
vases, columns, the rarest marbles, and a quantity of
other valuable articles were displayed without system or
order. These remains of luxury contrasted with the
simplicity adopted by the mistress of the house, with her
dress and her mode of life. Summer and winter Mme.
Du Barry wore only a dressing-robe of cotton cambric or
white muslin, and every day, whatever the weather
might be, she walked in her park, or outside of it, without
ever incurring disastrous consequences, so sturdy had
her health become through her life in the country. She
had maintained no relations with the numerous court
that surrounded her so long. In the evening we were
usually alone at the fireside, Mme. Du Barry and I. She
sometimes talked to me about Louis XV. and his court.
She showed herself a worthy person by her actions as well
as her words, and did a great deal of good at Louveciennes,
where she helped all the poor. Every day after dinner
we took coffee in the pavilion which was so famous for
its rich and tasteful decorations. The first time Mme.
Du Barry showed it to me she said: "It is here that
Louis XV. did me the honour of coming to dinner. There
was a gallery above for musicians and singers who performed during the meal."

When Mme. Du Barry went to England, before the Terror, to get back her stolen diamonds, which, in fact, she recovered there, the English received her very well. They did all they could to prevent her from returning to France. But it was not long before she succumbed to the fate in store for everybody who had some possessions. She was informed against and betrayed by a little Negro called Zamore, who is mentioned in all the memoirs of the period as having been overwhelmed with kindness by her and Louis XV. Being arrested and thrown into prison, Mme. Du Barry was tried and condemned to death by the Revolutionary tribunal at the end of 1793. She was the only woman, among all who perished in those dreadful days, unable to face the scaffold with firmness; she screamed, she sued for pardon to the hideous mob surrounding her, and that mob became moved to such a degree that the executioner hastened to finish his task. This has always confirmed my belief that if the victims of that period of execrable memory had not had the noble pride of dying with fortitude the Terror would have ceased long before it did.

I made three portraits of Mme. Du Barry. In the first I painted her at half length, in a dressing-gown and straw hat. In the second she is dressed in white satin; she holds a wreath in one hand, and one of her arms is leaning on a pedestal. The third portrait I made of Mme. Du Barry is in my own possession. I began it about the middle of September, 1789. From Louveciennes we could hear shooting in the distance, and I remember the poor woman saying, "If Louis XV. were alive I am sure this would not be happening." I had done the head, and outlined the body and arms, when I was obliged to make an expedition to Paris. I hoped to be able to return to Louveciennes to finish my work, but heard that Berthier and Foulon had been murdered. I was now frightened beyond measure, and thenceforth thought of nothing but leaving France. The fearful year 1789 was well advanced, and all decent people were already seized with terror. I remember perfectly that one evening when I had gathered some friends about me for a concert, most of the arrivals came into the room with looks of consternation; they had been walking at Longchamps that morning, and the populace assembled at the Etoile gate had cursed at those who passed in carriages in a dreadful manner. Some of the wretches had clambered on the carriage steps, shouting, "Next year you will be behind your carriages and we shall be inside !" and a thousand other insults.

As for myself, I had little need to learn fresh details in order to foresee what horrors impended. I knew beyond doubt that my house in the Rue Gros Chenet, where I had settled but three months since, had been singled out by the criminals. They threw sulphur into our cellars through the airholes. If I happened to be at my window, vulgar ruffians would shake their fists at me. Numberless sinister rumours reached me from every side; in fact, I now lived in a state of continual anxiety and sadness. My health became sensibly affected, and two of my best friends, the architect Brongniart and his wife, when they came to see me, found me so thin and so changed that they besought me to come and spend a few days with them, which invitation I thankfully accepted. Brongniart had his lodgings at the Invalides, whither I was conducted by a physician attached to the Palais Royal, whose servants wore the Orléans livery, the only one then held in any respect. There I was given everything of the best. As I was unable to eat, I was nourished on excellent Burgundy wine and soup, and Mme. Brongniart was in constant attendance upon me. All this solicitude ought to have quieted me, especially as my friends took a less black view of things than I did. Nevertheless, they did not succeed in banishing my evil forebodings. "What is the use of living; what is the use of taking care of one-self?" I would often ask my good friends, for the fears that the future held over me made life distasteful to me. But I must acknowledge that even with the furthest stretch of my imagination I guessed only at a fraction of the crimes that were to be committed.

I remember having supped at the Brongniarts's with His Excellence M. de Sombreuil, at that time governor of the Invalides. He brought us the news that an attempt was threatening to take the arms that he had in reserve, "But," he added, "I have hidden them so well that I defy any one to find them." The good man did not consider that one could trust no one but oneself. As the arms were very soon abstracted, it seems evident that he was betrayed by some of the servants in his employ.

M. de Sombreuil, as notable for his private virtues as for his military talents, was among the prisoners who were to be killed in their cells on the second of September. The murderers gave him his life at the tears of supplication of his heroic daughter, but, villainous even in granting pardon, they compelled Mlle. de Sombreuil to drink a glass of the blood that flowed in streams in front of the prison. For a long time afterward the sight of anything with red colour made this unfortunate young woman vomit horribly. Some years later (in 1794) M. de Sombreuil was sent to the scaffold by the Revolutionary tribunal.

I had made up my mind to leave France. For some years I had cherished the desire to go to Rome. The large number of portraits I had engaged to paint had, however, hindered me from putting my plan into execution. But I could now paint no longer; my broken spirit, bruised with so many horrors, shut itself entirely to my art. Besides, dreadful slanders were pouring upon my friends, my acquaintances and myself, although, Heaven

knows, I had never hurt a living soul. I thought like the
man who said, "I am accused of having stolen the
towers of Notre Dame; they are still in their usual place,
but I am going away, as I am evidently to blame." I
left several portraits I had begun, among them Mlle.
Contat's. At the same time I refused to paint Mlle.
de Laborde (afterward Duchess de Noailles), brought
to me by her father. She was scarcely sixteen, and
very charming, but it was no longer a question of success or money—it was only a question of saving one's
head. I had my carriage loaded, and my passport
ready, so that I might leave next day with my daughter
and her governess, when a crowd of national guardsmen
burst into my room with their muskets. Most of them
were drunk and shabby, and had terrible faces. A
few of them came up to me and told me in the coarsest
language that I must not go, but that I must remain.
I answered that since everybody had been called upon
to enjoy his liberty, I intended to make use of mine.
They would barely listen to me, and kept on repeating,
"You will not go, citizeness; you will not go!" Finally
they went away. I was plunged into a state of cruel
anxiety when I saw two of them return. But they
did not frighten me, although they belonged to the gang,
so quickly did I recognise that they wished me no harm.
"Madame," said one of them, "we are your neighbours,
and we have come to advise you to leave, and as soon as
possible. You cannot live here; you are changed so
much that we feel sorry for you. But do not go in your
carriage: go in the stage-coach; it is much safer." I
thanked them with all my heart, and followed their
good advice. I had three places reserved, as I still
wanted to take my daughter, who was then five or six
years old, but was unable to secure them until a fortnight
later, because all who exiled themselves chose the stage-
coach, like myself. At last came the long-expected day.

It was the 5th of October, and the King and Queen were conducted from Versailles to Paris surrounded by pikes. The events of that day filled me with uneasiness as to the fate of Their Majesties and that of all decent people, so that I was dragged to the stage-coach at midnight in a dreadful state of mind. I was very much afraid of the Faubourg Saint Antoine, which I was obliged to traverse to reach the Barrière du Trône. My brother and my husband escorted me as far as this gate without leaving the door of the coach for a moment; but the suburb that I was so frightened of was perfectly quiet. All its inhabitants, the workmen and the rest, had been to Versailles after the royal family, and fatigue kept them all in bed.

Opposite me in the coach was a very filthy man, who stunk like the plague, and told me quite simply that he had stolen watches and other things. Luckily he saw nothing about me to tempt him, for I was only taking a small amount of clothing and eighty louis for my journey. I had left my principal effects and my jewels in Paris, and the fruit of my labours was in the hands of my husband, who spent it all. I lived abroad solely on the proceeds of my painting.

Not satisfied with relating his fine exploits to us, the thief talked incessantly of stringing up such and such people on lamp-posts, naming a number of my own acquaintances. My daughter thought this man very wicked. He frightened her, and this gave me the courage to say, "I beg you, sir, not to talk of killing before this child." That silenced him, and he ended by playing at battle with my daughter. On the bench I occupied there also sat a mad Jacobin from Grenoble, about fifty years old, with an ugly, bilious complexion, who each time we stopped at an inn for dinner or supper made violent speeches of the most fearful kind. At all of the towns a crowd of people stopped the coach to learn

the news from Paris.   Our Jacobin would then exclaim:
"Everything is going well, children! We have the baker
and his wife safe in Paris.   A constitution will be drawn
up, they will be forced to accept it, and then it will be
all over."   There were plenty of ninnies and flatheads
who believed this man as if he had been an oracle.   All
this made my journey a very melancholy one.   I had
no further fears for myself, but I feared greatly for everybody else—for my mother, for my brother, and for my
friends.   I also had the gravest apprehensions concerning
Their Majesties, for all along the route, nearly as far
as Lyons, men on horseback rode up to the coach to tell
us that the King and Queen had been killed and that
Paris was on fire.   My poor little girl got all a-tremble;
she thought she saw her father dead and our house
burned down, and no sooner had I succeeded in reassuring
her than another horseman appeared and told us the
same stories.

I cannot describe the emotions I felt in passing over
the Beauvoisin Bridge.   Then only did I breathe freely.
I had left France behind, that France which nevertheless
was the land of my birth, and which I reproached myself
with quitting with so much satisfaction.   The sight of
the mountains, however, distracted me from all my sad
thoughts.   I had never seen high mountains before;
those of the Savoy seemed to touch the sky, and seemed
to mingle with it in a thick vapour.   My first sensation
was that of fear, but I unconsciously accustomed myself
to the spectacle, and ended by admiring it.   A certain
part of the road completely entranced me; I seemed to
see the "Gallery of the Titans," and I have always called
it so since.   Wishing to enjoy all these beauties as fully
as possible, I got down from the coach, but after
walking some way I was seized with a great
fright, for there were explosions being made with
gunpowder, which had the effect of a thousand cannon

shots, and the din echoing from rock to rock was truly
infernal.

I went up Mount Cenis, as other strangers were doing,
when a postilion approached me, saying, "The lady
ought to take a mule; to climb up on foot is too
fatiguing." I answered that I was a work-woman and
quite accustomed to walking. "Oh! no!" was the
laughing reply. "The lady is no work-woman; we know
who she is!" "Well, who am I, then?" I asked him.
"You are Mme. Lebrun, who paints so well, and we
are all very glad to see you safe from those bad
people." I never guessed how the man could have
learned my name, but it proved to me how many
secret agents the Jacobins must have had. Happily
I had no occasion to fear them any longer.

No sooner had I arrived at Rome than I did a portrait
of myself for the Florence gallery. I painted myself
palette in hand before a canvas on which I was tracing
a figure of the Queen in white crayon. After that I
painted Miss Pitt, who was sixteen and extremely pretty.
I represented her as Hebe, on some clouds, holding in
her hand a goblet from which an eagle was about to
drink. I did the eagle from life, and I thought he would
eat me. He belonged to Cardinal de Bernis. The
wretched beast, accustomed to being in the open air—
for he was kept on a chain in the courtyard—was so
enraged at finding himself in my room that he tried to
fly at me. I admit that I was dreadfully frightened.

About this time I painted the portrait of a Polish
lady, the Countess Potocka. She came with her husband,
and after he had gone away she said to me quite coolly,
"He is my third husband, but I am thinking of taking
back my first, who would suit me better, although he
is a drunkard." I painted this Pole in a very picturesque
way: for a background she had a rock overgrown with
moss, and falling water nearby.

The pleasure of living in Rome was the only thing that consoled me for having left my country, my family, and so many friends I loved. My work did not deprive me of the daily diversion of going about the city and its surroundings. I always went alone to the palaces where collections of pictures and statues were exhibited, so as not to have my enjoyment spoiled by stupid remarks or questions. All these palaces are open to strangers, and much gratitude is due to the great Roman nobles for being so obliging. It may seem hard to believe, but it is true that one might spend one's whole life in the palaces and churches. In the churches are to be found great treasures of painting and extraordinary monuments. The wealth of St. Peter's in this respect is well known. The finest of the churches regarding architecture is St. Paul's, whose interior is lined with columns on each side.

One can have no idea of the grand and imposing effect of the Catholic religion unless one can see Rome during Lent. On Easter Day I took good care to be in the square of St. Peter's to see the Pope give his blessing. Nothing could have been more solemn. The immense square was filled at early morning by peasants and by the inhabitants of the town, in all sorts of different costumes—bright and varied in colour—and there were also a large number of pilgrims. They all stood as still as the superb obelisk of Oriental granite in the middle of the square. At ten o'clock the Pope arrived, clothed all in white, his crown on his head. He took his place in the centre stand outside the church on a magnificent high velvet throne. The Cardinals surrounded him, clad in their handsome dress. It must be said that Pope Pius VI. was splendid. His healthy face showed no sign of the wear and tear of old age. His hands were white and plump. He knelt down to read his prayer. Afterward, rising up, he gave a double blessing in speaking these words, *"Urbi et Orbi."* Then, as if struck by an electric shock, the people, the strangers, the troops, and all others fell on their knees, while the cannons boomed from all sides, this adding to the majesty of the scene, by which it was impossible not to be moved.

The blessing given, the Cardinals threw a quantity of papers down from the gallery, and these, I was told, were indulgences. Thousands of hands shot upward to grasp them. The eagerness and the excitement of this crowd, its pressing and pushing, were beyond description. When the Pope withdrew, the regimental bands intoned a flourish, and the troops then marched off to the rattle of drums. In the evening the dome of St. Peter's was illuminated, first with lights under coloured glasses, and then with white lights of greatest brilliancy. It was difficult to conceive how the change could be effected with such rapidity; however, the spectacle was as beautiful as it was remarkable. The same evening, too, gorgeous fireworks were set off at the castle of St. Angelo. Myriads of bombs and fire balloons were sent into the air; the final display was the most magnificent to be seen of the kind, and the reflection of these splendid fireworks in the Tiber doubled their effect.

In Rome, where everything is grand, the great mansions have no wretched lamps before them, but each palace is provided with enormous candelabras, from which stream gigantic flames that shed day, so to speak, over the whole city. This luxurious manner of lighting strikes a stranger the more as the streets of Rome are mostly illuminated by the lamps burning in front of the Madonnas.

Strangers are attracted to Rome far more by Holy Week than by the carnival, at which I was not surprised. The masqueraders establish themselves in tiers, disguised as harlequins, as pulcinellos, etc., just as we see

them on the boulevards in Paris, the difference being
that in Rome they never stir. I saw only a single young
man going about the streets after the French fashion.
He was giving a lifelike imitation of a very affected
exquisite whom we had no difficulty in recognising.
The carriages and wagons come and go full of richly
costumed people. The horses are adorned with feathers,
ribbons, and bells, the servants being dressed up as
Scaramouche or Harlequin, but it all passes off in the
quietest way in the world. Finally, toward evening,
several discharges of cannon announce the horse-races,
which enliven the rest of the day.

There is no town in the world where one could pass
one's time as delightfully as in Rome, even were one
deprived of all the resources which good society offers.
The walks within the walls are a joy, for one is never
tired of revisiting the Coliseum, the Capitol, the
Pantheon, the square of St. Peter's with its colonnades,
its superb obelisk, and its lovely fountains, across which
the rays of the sun often throw beautiful rainbows. The
square is wonderfully impressive at sunset and in the
moonlight. Whether it was on my way or not, I always
took pleasure in crossing it.

What astonished me very much in Rome was to find
at the Coliseum, on Sunday mornings, a crowd of women
from the lowest classes, extravagantly bedizened, loaded
with ornaments, and wearing in their ears enormous
stars of paste diamonds. It was also in this garb that
they went to church, frequently followed by a domestic,
who very often was no other than their husband, his
real occupation being probably that of a valet. These
women do nothing at home; their idleness is such that
they live in the greatest want. They may be seen at
their windows in the streets of Rome, with flowers and
feathers on their head, their faces made up with cosmetics.
The upper part of their dress, which is visible, indicates

great luxury, so that one is surprised, upon entering their rooms, to find that they have on nothing more than a dirty petticoat. The Roman dames whom I mention nevertheless enact aristocratic parts, and when the time comes to go to the villas they carefully close their shutters in order to create the belief that they have left for the country.

I was assured that every woman in Rome was in the habit of carrying a dagger. I do not, however, believe that the great ladies wear any, but certain it is that the wife of Denis, the landscape painter, with whom I lodged, and who was a Roman, showed me the dagger which she always had about her. As for the men of the people, they are never unprovided with one, and this brings about a number of grave tragedies. Three evenings after my arrival, for instance, I heard in my street some shouts followed by a great tumult. I sent out to learn what the matter was, and was informed that a man had just killed another with his dagger. As these peculiar habits made me very much afraid, I was assured that strangers had nothing to fear—that it was simply a question of an act of revenge between Italians. As for the case in point, the murderer and his victim had quarrelled ten years ago, and the first, having recognised his enemy, at once struck him down with his dagger, which proves how long an Italian can keep a grudge.

Certainly the customs of the upper class are milder, since high society is very much the same all over Europe. However, I am not the best judge, as with the exception of relations involving my art, and invitations sent to me for numerous parties, I had little occasion to become acquainted with the patrician ladies of Rome. What happened to me was what naturally happens to every exile, which was to seek the company of my own countrymen. In 1789 and 1790 Rome was full of French refugees, whom I knew for the greater part, and with whom I soon made friends. We saw the Princess Joseph de Monaco and the Duchess de Fleury arrive, and a host of other notabilities. The Princess Joseph de Monaco had a charming face, and was very sweet and charming. Unfortunately for her, she did not stay in Rome. She returned to Paris to attend to the small amount of property remaining to her children, and she was there during the Terror. Thrown into prison and condemned to death, she was taken to the scaffold.

The arrival at Rome of so many people bringing so much news made me undergo different emotions every day. Often they were very sad, but sometimes very sweet. I was told, for instance, that a little while after my departure, when the King was begged to have his picture painted, he had replied: "No, I shall wait for Mme. Lebrun to come back, so that she may make a portrait of me to match the Queen's. I want her to paint me at full figure, in the act of commanding M. de la Perouse to make a journey round the world."

CHAPTER V

Neapolitan Days

I HAD been in Rome eight months or thereabouts, when,
observing that all foreigners were leaving for Naples,
I was seized with a great desire to go there likewise.
I confided my plan to the Cardinal de Bernis, who, while
approving, advised me not to go alone. He spoke to
me of a M. Duvivier, the husband of Voltaire's niece,
Mme. Denis, who proposed to make the journey, and
who would be charmed with my company. M. Duvivier
came to me, repeating everything that the Cardinal
had said, and promising to take care of my daughter
and myself. He added, thus tempting me the more,
that he had in his carriage a sort of stove, for cooking
fowl, which would be very useful to us, seeing how bad
the fare was in the best inns of Terracina. All his
offers suited me to a marvel, and so I started with this
gentleman. His coach was very large; my daughter
and her governess sat in front, and there was another
seat in the middle. A huge man-servant sat on it in
front of me in such a way that his large back touched

me and I had to hold my nose.   I am not in the habit
of talking while travelling, so that conversation between
us was restricted to the exchange of a few phrases.   But
as we were crossing the Pontine marshes, I noticed on
the edge of a canal a shepherd whose flock was passing
into a meadow all studded with flowers, and beyond
which the sea and Cape Circe were visible.   " What a
charming picture !" said I to my travelling companion.
"This shepherd, these sheep, the meadow, the sea !"
"Those sheep are all filthy," he answered; "you ought
to see them in England."   Farther along on the Terracina
road, at the place where you cross a small river in a
boat, I saw at my left the line of the Apennines crowned
with magnificent clouds, which the setting sun illumined.
I was unable to refrain from expressing my admiration
aloud.   "Those clouds mean that we shall have rain
to-morrow," said my optimistic friend.

We reached Naples at about three or four o'clock.
I cannot describe the impression I received upon entering
the town.   That burning sun, that stretch of sea, those
islands seen in the distance, that Vesuvius with a great
column of smoke ascending from it, and the very population so animated and so noisy, who differ so much
from the Roman that one might suppose they were a
thousand miles apart.

I had engaged a house at Chiaja on the edge of the
sea. Opposite me I had the island of Capri, and this
situation delighted me.   Hardly had I arrived when
Count Skavronska, the Russian Ambassador at Naples,
whose house was next to mine, sent one of his runners
to find out how I was, and at the same time had a very
choice dinner brought me.   I was the more grateful for
this kind attention, as I must have died of hunger before
there would have been time to get my kitchen ready.
The same evening I went to thank the Count, and thus
became acquainted with his charming wife.

Count Skavronska had features that were noble and regular; he was very pale. This pallor came from the extreme delicacy of his health, which, however, did not prevent him from being highly sociable nor from chatting both gracefully and cleverly. The Countess was as sweet and pretty as an angel. The famous Potemkin, her uncle, had loaded her with wealth, for which she had no use. Her great delight was to live stretched out on a lounge wrapped in a large black cloak, and wearing no stays. Her mother-in-law sent her, from Paris, cases full of the most beautiful dresses then made by Mlle. Bertin, Queen Marie Antoinette's dressmaker. I do not believe that the Countess ever opened one of them, and when her mother-in-law expressed a wish to see her in the beautiful gowns and head-dresses contained in the cases, she answered indifferently: "What for? Why?" She gave me the same answer when showing me her jewel-case, one of the most splendid I have ever seen. It contained enormous diamonds given her by Potemkin, but I never saw them on her. I remember her telling me that in order to go to sleep she had a slave under her bed who told her the same story every night. She was utterly idle all day, she had no education, and her conversation was quite empty. But in spite of all that, thanks to her lovely face and her angelic sweetness, she had an incomparable charm.

Count Skavronska had made me promise to do his wife's portrait before any one else's, and, having agreed, I began this portrait two days after my arrival. After the first session, Sir William Hamilton, the British Ambassador at Naples, came to me and begged that my first portrait in this town should be that of the splendid woman he presented to me. This was Mme. Harte, who soon after became Lady Hamilton, and who was famous for her beauty. After the promise to my amiable neighbours, I could not begin the other portrait until

Countess Skavronska's was well advanced. I then painted Mme. Harte as a bacchante reclining by the edge of the sea, holding a goblet in her hand. Her beautiful face had much animation, and was a complete contrast to the Countess's. She had a great quantity of fine chestnut hair, sufficient to cover her entirely, and thus, as a bacchante with flying hair, she was admirable to behold.

The life of Lady Hamilton is a romance. Her maiden name was Emma Lyon. Her mother, it is said, was a poor servant, and there is some disagreement as to her birthplace. At the age of thirteen she entered the service of an honest townsman of Hawarden as a nurse, but, tired of the dull life she led, and believing that she could obtain a more agreeable situation in London, she betook herself thither. The Prince of Wales told me that he had seen her at that time in wooden shoes at the stall of a fruit vender, and that, although she was very meanly clad, her pretty face attracted attention. A shopkeeper took her into his service, but she soon left him to become housemaid under a lady of decent family—a very respectable person. In her house she acquired a taste for novels, and then for the play. She studied the gestures and vocal inflections of the actors, and rendered them with remarkable facility. These talents, neither of which pleased her mistress in the very least, were the cause of her dismissal. It was then that, having heard of a tavern where painters were in the habit of meeting, she conceived the idea of going there to look for employment. Her beauty was then at its height.

She was rescued from this pitfall by a strange chance. Doctor Graham took her to exhibit her at his house, covered with a light veil, as the goddess Hygeia (the goddess of health). A number of curious people and amateurs went to see her, and the painters were especially delighted. Some time after this exhibition, a painter secured her as a model; he made her pose in a thousand graceful attitudes, which he reproduced on canvas. She now perfected herself in this new sort of talent which made her famous. Nothing, indeed, was more remarkable than the ease Lady Hamilton acquired in spontaneously giving her features an expression of sorrow or of joy, and of posing marvellously to represent different people. Her eyes a-kindle, her hair flying, she showed you a bewitching bacchante; then, all of a sudden, her face expressed grief, and you saw a magnificent repentant Magdalen. The day her husband presented her to me, she insisted on my seeing her in a pose. I was delighted, but she was dressed in every-day clothes, which gave me a shock. I had gowns made for her such as I wore in order to paint in comfort, and which consisted of a kind of loose tunic. She also took some shawls to drape herself with, which she understood very well, and then was ready to render enough different positions and expressions to fill a whole picture gallery. There is, in fact, a collection drawn by Frederic Reimberg, which has been engraved.

To return to the romance of Emma Lyon. It was while she was with the painter I have mentioned that Lord Greville fell so desperately in love with her that he intended to marry her, when he suddenly lost his official place and was ruined. He at once left for Naples in the hope of obtaining help from his Uncle Hamilton, and took Emma with him so that she might plead his cause. The uncle, indeed, consented to pay all his nephew's debts, but also decided to marry Emma Lyon in spite of his family's remonstrances. Lady Hamilton became as great a lady as can be imagined. It is asserted that the Queen of Naples was on an intimate footing with her. Certain it is that the Queen saw her often— politically, might perhaps be said. Lady Hamilton,

being a most indiscreet woman, betrayed a number
of little diplomatic secrets to the Queen, of which she
made use to the advantage of her country.

Lady Hamilton was not at all clever, though she was
extremely supercilious and disdainful, so much so that
these two defects were conspicuous in all her conversation.
But she also possessed considerable craftiness, of which
she made use in order to bring about her marriage. She
wanted in style, and dressed very badly when it was a
question of every-day dress. I remember that when I
did my first picture of her, as a sibyl, she was living at
Caserta, whither I went every day, desiring to progress
quickly with the picture. The Duchess de Fleury and
the Princess de Joseph Monaco were present at the third
sitting, which was the last. I had wound a scarf round
her head in the shape of a turban, one end hanging down
in graceful folds. This head-dress so beautified her that
the ladies declared she looked ravishing. Her husband
having invited us all to dinner, she went to her apartment to change, and when she came back to meet us in
the drawing-room, her new costume, which was a very
ordinary one indeed, had so altered her to her disadvantage that the two ladies had all the difficulty in the
world in recognising her.

When I went to London in 1802 Lady Hamilton had
just lost her husband. I left a card for her, and she soon
came to see me, wearing deep mourning, with a dense
black veil surrounding her, and she had had her splendid
hair cut off to follow the new "Titus" fashion. I found
this Andromache enormous, for she had become terribly
fat. She said that she was very much to be pitied, that
in her husband she had lost a friend and a father, and
that she would never be consoled. I confess that her
grief made little impression upon me, since it seemed to
me that she was playing a part. I was evidently not
mistaken, because a few minutes later, having noticed

some music lying on my piano, she took up a lively tune and began to sing it.

As is well known, Lord Nelson had been in love with her at Naples; she had maintained a very tender correspondence with him. When I went to return her visit one morning, I found her radiant with joy, and besides she had put a rose in her hair, like Nina. I could not help asking her what the rose signified. "It is because I have just received a letter from Lord Nelson," she answered.

The Duke de Berri and the Duke de Bourbon, having heard of her poses, very much desired to witness a spectacle which she had never been willing to offer in London. I requested her to give me an evening for the two Princes, and she consented. I also invited some other French people, who I was aware would be anxious to see this sight. On the day appointed I placed in the middle of my drawing-room a very large frame, with a screen on either side of it. I had had a strong limelight prepared and disposed so that it could not be seen, but which would light up Lady Hamilton as though she were a picture. All the invited guests having arrived, Lady Hamilton assumed various attitudes in this frame in a truly admirable way. She had brought a little girl with her, who might have been seven or eight years old, and who resembled her strikingly. One group they made together reminded me of Poussin's "Rape of the Sabines." She changed from grief to joy and from joy to terror so rapidly and effectively that we were all enchanted. As I kept her for supper, the Duke de Bourbon, who sat next to me at table, called my attention to the quantity of porter she drank. I am sure she must have been used to it, for she was not tipsy after two or three bottles. Long after leaving London, in 1815, I heard that Lady Hamilton had ended her days at Calais, dying there neglected and forsaken in the most awful poverty.

The excursions I made at Naples did not prevent me

from accomplishing a great deal of work. I even undertook so many portraits that my first stay in that town
extended to six months. I had arrived with the intention
of spending only six weeks. The French Ambassador, the
Baron de Talleyrand, came to inform me one morning
that the Queen of Naples wished me to do the portraits of
her two eldest daughters, and I began upon them at once.
Her Majesty was preparing to leave for Vienna, where
she was to busy herself about the marriage of these
Princesses. I remember her saying to me after her
return: "I have had a successful journey; I have just
made two fortunate matches for my daughters." The
eldest, in fact, soon after was married to the Emperor
of Austria, Francis II., and the other, who was called
Louise, to the Grand Duke of Tuscany. This second
girl was very ugly, and made such grimaces that I did
not want to finish her picture. She died a few years
after her marriage.

During the Queen's absence I also painted the Prince
Royal. The hour of noon was appointed for the sittings,
and in order to attend I was obliged to follow the Chiaja
road in the heat of the day. The houses on the left, which
faced the sea, being painted a lustrous white, the sun was
reflected from them so vividly that I was almost struck
blind. To save my eyes, I put on a green veil, which I
had never seen any one else do, and which must have
looked rather peculiar, since only black or white veils were
worn. But a few days after I saw several English women
imitating me, and green veils came into fashion. I also
found great comfort in my green veil at St. Petersburg,
where the snow was so dazzling that it might have killed
my eyesight.

One of my greatest pleasures was to go for walks on
the lovely slope of Posilippo. Under it is the grotto of
the same name, which is a splendid piece of work a mile
long, and which is recognised as having been done by the

Romans. This slope of Posilippo is covered with country houses, casinos, meadows, and very fine trees with vines winding about them in festoons. It is here that Virgil's tomb is to be found, and it is said that laurels grow upon it, but I must confess that I saw none. In the evenings I walked on the seashore; I frequently took my daughter, and we often remained sitting there together until moon-rise, enjoying the salubrious air and the gorgeous view. This was a rest for my daughter after her daily studies, for I had resolved to give her the best education possible, and to this effect I had engaged at Naples masters of writing, geography, Italian, English, and German. She showed a preference for German above the others, and evinced a remarkable aptitude in her various studies. There were some signs in her of a talent for painting, but her favourite pastime was to compose novels. Returning from evening parties to which I had gone, I would find her with a pen in her hand and another in her cap; I would then oblige her to go to bed, but not infrequently did she secretly get up in the middle of the night to finish one of her chapters, and I remember very well how, at the age of nine, at Vienna, she wrote a little romance as remarkable for its situations as for its style.

All the portraits I had engaged to do at Naples being finished, I went back to Rome, but hardly had I arrived when the Queen of Naples arrived also, she making a stop there on her return journey from Vienna. As I happened to be in the crowd through which she made her way, she noticed me and spoke to me, and begged me with extreme graciousness to visit Naples once more for the purpose of painting her portrait. It was impossible to refuse, and I complied with her wish at once.

Upon arriving at Naples I began the portrait of the Queen forthwith. It was then so terribly hot that one day when Her Majesty gave me a sitting we both fell

asleep. I took great pleasure in doing this picture.
The Queen of Naples, without being as pretty as her
younger sister, the Queen of France, reminded me strongly
of her. Her face was worn, but one readily judged that
she had been handsome; her hands and arms especially
were perfect in form and colour. This Princess, of whom
so much evil has been written and spoken, had an affectionate nature and simple ways at home. Her magna-
nimity was truly royal. The Marquis de Bombelles, the
Ambassador at Vienna in 1790, was the only French
envoy who refused to swear to the constitution; the Queen,
being apprised that by this brave and noble conduct
M. de Bombelles, the father of a large family, had been
reduced to the most unfortunate position, wrote him a
letter of commendation with her own hand. She added
that all sovereigns should be at one in acknowledging
faithful subjects, and asked him to accept a pension of
twelve thousand francs. She had a fine character and a
good deal of wit. She bore the burden of government
alone. The King would have nothing to do with it; he
spent most of his time at Caserta. Before I left
Naples for good the Queen presented me with a box of
old lacquer, with her initials surrounded by beautiful
diamonds. The initials are worth ten thousand francs;
I shall keep them all my life.

I had a burning desire to see Venice; I arrived there
the day before Ascension. M. Denon, whom I had known
in Paris, having heard of this, came to see me without
delay. His cleverness and his great knowledge of the arts
made him the most charming mentor, and I congratulated
myself upon such a happy encounter. The very next day
he took me out on the canal, where the marriage of the
Doge with the sea was enacted. The Doge and all the
members of the senate were on a vessel gilded inside and
out and called the *Bucentaur;* it was surrounded
by a swarm of boats, of which several were occupied by

musicians. The Doge and the senators had on black gowns and white wigs with three bows. When the *Bucentaur* had reached the place fixed for the celebration of the marriage, the Doge pulled a ring from his finger and threw it into the sea. At the same instant a thousand cannon shots announced to the city and its surroundings the consummation of this great wedding, which concluded with mass.

A number of strangers were present at the ceremony. I observed among them Prince Augustus of England, and the charming Princess Joseph de Monaco, then preparing to go back to France for her children. I saw her at Venice for the last time.

CHAPTER VI

Turin and Vienna

A QUEEN WHO REFUSED TO BE PAINTED — A FOUR-
COURSE DINNER OF FROGS, FROGS, FROGS AND FROGS —
VILLEGGIATURA — FRENCH REFUGEES AT TURIN —
THEIR HEARTRENDING PLIGHT — VIENNA — NEWS OF
THE "AWFUL MURDER" OF LOUIS XVI. AND MARIE
ANTOINETTE — BAREFOOT PRINCESS LICHTENSTEIN —
INDUCEMENTS TO VISIT RUSSIA — JOURNEY THITHER
VIA DRESDEN — THE SISTINE MADONNA.

MEANWHILE, it being my desire to see France again, I
reached Turin with this end in view. The two aunts
of Louis XVI. had been kind enough to give me letters
to Clotilda, Queen of Sardinia, their niece. They sent
word that they very much wished to have a portrait
done by me, and consequently, as soon as I was settled,
I presented myself before Her Majesty. She received
me very well after reading the letters of Princess Adelaide
and Princess Victoria. She told me that she regretted
having to refuse her aunts, but that, having renounced
the world altogether, she must decline being painted.
What I saw indeed seemed quite in accord with her
statement and her resolve. The Queen of Sardinia had
her hair cut short and wore on her head a little cap,
which, like the rest of her garb, was the simplest con-
ceivable. Her leanness struck me particularly, as I had
seen her when she was very young, before her marriage,
when her stoutness was so pronounced that she was

74

called "Fat Milady" in France. Be it that this change was caused by too austere religious practices, or by the sufferings which the misfortunes of her family had made her undergo, the fact was that she had altered beyond recognition. The King joined her in the room where she received me. He was likewise so pale and thin that it was painful to look at them together.

I lost no time in going to see Madame, the wife of Louis XVIII. She not only accorded me a warm welcome, but arranged picturesque drives for me in the neighbourhood of Turin, which I took with her lady-in-waiting, Mme. de Gourbillon, and her son. Said surroundings are very beautiful, but our first expedition was not very auspicious. We set out in the heat of the day to visit a monastery situated high up on a mountain. As the mountain was very steep, we were obliged to get out of the carriage when we had gone half way and then climb on foot. I remember passing a spring of the clearest water, whose drops sparkled like diamonds, and which peasants declared to be a cure for sundry diseases. After climbing so long that we were exhausted, we at length arrived at the monastery dying with heat and hunger. The table was already laid for the monks and for travellers, which filled us with joy, since it may be imagined how impatient we were for dinner. As there was some delay, we thought that something special was being done for us, seeing that Madame had recommended us to the monks in a letter she had given us addressed to them. At last a dish of frogs' breasts was served, which I took for a chicken stew. But as soon as I tasted it I found it impossible to eat another morsel, hungry as I was. Then three other dishes were brought on, boiled, fried and grilled, and I set great hopes on each in turn. Alas! they were only frogs again! So we ate nothing but dry bread, and drank water, these monks never drinking nor offering wine. My heart's

desire was then an omelet—but there were no eggs in
the house.

After my visit to the monastery I met Porporati,
who wanted me to live with him.. He proposed occupying
a farm he owned two miles from Turin, where he had
some plain but comfortable rooms. I gladly accepted
this offer, as I hated living in town, and at once went
to establish myself with my daughter and her governess
in this retreat. The farm stood in the open country,
surrounded with fields, and little streams edged by trees
high enough to form delightful bowers. From morning
till night I took rapturous walks in these enchanting
solitudes. My child enjoyed the pure air as much as
I did the quiet, peaceful life that we led. Alas! it was
in this peaceful place, while I was in such a happy state
of mind, that I was struck a most cruel blow. The
cart which brought our letters having come one evening,
the carter handed me one from my friend M. de Rivière,
my sister-in-law's brother, who apprised me of the
dreadful events of the 10th of August and supplied me
with some horrible details. I was quite overcome, and
made up my mind to go back to Turin immediately.

On entering the town, great heavens! what did I
behold! Streets, squares, were all filled with men and
women of all ages who had fled from French towns and
come to Turin in search of a home. They were coming
in by thousands, and the sight broke my heart. Most
of them brought neither baggage, nor money, nor even
food, for they had had no time to do anything but think
been of saving their lives. Since then the case has been
cited to me of the aged Duchess de Villeroi, whose lady's
maid, possessing a small sum of money, kept her alive
on the way by a daily expenditure of ten sous. The
children were crying with hunger in lamentable fashion.
In fact, I never saw anything more pitiful. The King
of Sardinia ordered these unfortunates to be housed and

fed, but there was not room for all. Madame also did much to succour them; we went all over the town, accompanied by her equerry, seeking lodgings and victuals for the poor wretches, without being able to find as many of either as were wanted.

Never shall I forget the impression made upon me by an old soldier, decorated with the cross of St. Louis, who might have been about sixty-five years old. He was a fine man with a noble mien, supporting himself against the curbstone at the corner of a lonely street; he accosted nobody and asked for nothing; I believe he would rather have died of hunger than beg, but the profound unhappiness imprinted on his face compelled interest at first sight. We went straight to him, giving him a little money that remained to us, and he thanked us with sobs in his throat. The next day he was lodged in the King's palace, as several other refugees were, for there was no more room in the town.

It may well be imagined that I abandoned the plan of going to Paris. I decided to leave for Vienna instead.

Vienna is of considerable extent, if you count its thirty-two suburbs. It is full of very fine palaces. The Imperial Museum boasts pictures by the greatest masters, and I often went to admire them, as well as those belonging to Prince Lichtenstein. His gallery comprises seven rooms, of which one contains only pictures by Van Dyck and the others some fine Titians, Caravaggios, Rubens, Canalettos, and so on. There are also several masterpieces by the last-named painter in the Imperial Museum.

It has been said with truth that the Prater is one of the best promenades in existence. It is a long, magnificent avenue in which large numbers of elegant carriages drive up and down, and which is lined on either side by sitting spectators, just as in the great avenue of the Tuileries. But what renders the Prater more pleasant

and more picturesque is that the avenue leads to a wood,
which is not very thick, and full of deer so tame that
one can approach them without frightening them.
There is another promenade on the bank of the Danube,
where every Sunday various companies of the middle
classes meet together to eat fried chicken. The park of
Schoenbrunn is also well frequented, especially on
Sundays. Its broad avenues, and the pretty resting
places on the heights at the end of the park, make it
very pleasant for walking in.

In Vienna I went to several balls, especially to those
given by the Russian Ambassador, Count Rasomovski.
They danced the waltz there with such fury that I could
not imagine how all these people, spinning round at
such a rate, did not fall down from giddiness; but men
and women were so accustomed to this violent exercise
that they never rested a single moment while a ball
lasted. The "polonaise" was often danced, too, and
was much less fatiguing, for this dance is nothing more
than a procession in which you quietly walk two by
two. It suits pretty women to perfection, as there is
time to look their faces and figures all over.

I also wanted to see a great court ball. I was invited
to one. The Emperor Francis II. had taken for his
second wife Maria Theresa of the two Sicilies, daughter
to the Queen of Naples. I had painted this Princess
in 1792, but I found her so changed on meeting her at
this ball that I had difficulty in recognising her. Her
nose had lengthened, and her cheeks had sunk so much
that she resembled her father. I was sorry for her
sake that she had not kept her mother's features, who
reminded me strongly of our charming Queen of France.

A person whose friendship I had great pleasure in
renewing at Vienna was the Countess de Brionne, Princess
de Lorraine. She had been most kind to me in my
early youth, and I resumed the agreeable habit of supping

at her house, where I often met the valiant Prince Nassau, so formidable in a fight, so gentle and modest in a *salon*.

I also made frequent visits at the house of the Countess de Rombec, sister of Count Cobentzel. The Countess de Rombec gathered about her the most distinguished society of Vienna. It was under her roof that I saw Prince Metternich and his son, who has since become prime minister, and who was then nothing but a very handsome young man. I there met again the amiable Prince de Ligne; he told us about the delightful journey he had made in the Crimea with the Empress Catherine II., and inspired me with a wish to see that great ruler. In the same house I encountered the Duchess de Guiche, whose lovely face had not changed in the least. Her mother, the Duchess de Polignac, lived permanently at a place near Vienna. It was there that she heard of the death of Louis XVI., which affected her health very seriously, but when she heard the dreadful news of the Queen's death she succumbed altogether. Her grief changed her to such an extent that her pretty face became unrecognisable, and every one foresaw that she had not much longer to live. She did, in fact, die in a little while, leaving her family and some friends who would not leave her disconsolate at their loss.

I can judge how terrible that which had happened in France must have been to her by the sorrow I experienced myself. I learned nothing from the newspapers, for I had read them no more since the day when, having opened one at Mme. de Rombec's, I had found the names of nine persons of my acquaintance who had been guillotined. People even took care to hide all political pamphlets from me. I thus heard of the horrible occurrence through my brother, who wrote it down and sent the letter without giving any further particulars whatever. His heart broken, he simply wrote that Louis XVI. and

Marie Antoinette had perished on the scaffold. Afterward, from compassion toward myself, I always abstained from putting the least question concerning what accompanied or preceded that awful murder, so that I should have known nothing about it to this very day had it not been for a certain fact to which I may possibly refer in the future.

As soon as spring came I took a little house in a village near Vienna and went to settle there. This village, called Huitzing, was adjacent to the park of Schoenbrunn. I took with me to Huitzing the large portrait I was then doing of the Princess Lichtenstein, to finish it. This young Princess was very well built; her pretty face had a sweet, angelic expression, which gave me the idea of representing her as Iris. I painted her standing, as if about to fly into the air. She had about her a fluttering, rainbow-coloured scarf. Of course I painted her with naked feet, but when the picture was hung in her husband's gallery the heads of the family were greatly scandalised at seeing the Princess exhibited without shoes, and the Prince told me that he had had a pair of nice, little slippers placed under the portrait, which slippers, so he had informed the grandparents, had slipped off her feet and fallen on the ground.

At Vienna I was as happy as any one possibly could be away from her kin and country. In the winter the city offered one of the most agreeable and brilliant societies of Europe, and when the fine weather returned I delightedly sought my little country retreat. Not thinking of leaving Austria before I could safely return to France, the Russian Ambassador and some of his compatriots urged me strongly to go to St. Petersburg, where, they assured me, the Empress would be pleased to see me. Everything that the Prince de Ligne had told me about Catherine II. inspired me with an irrepressible desire to get a glance at that potentate. Moreover I reasoned correctly that even a short stay in Russia would complete the fortune I had decided to make before resuming residence in Paris. So I made up my mind to go.

After a sojourn at Vienna of two years and a half, I left that place in April of the year 1795 for Prague. I then passed on to Budweis, whose surroundings are most engaging. The town is deserted, the fortifications are in ruins; there are only old men and some women and children to be met with—and not many of those. Finally we reached Dresden by a very narrow road skirting the Elbe at a great height, the river flowing through a broad valley. The very day after my arrival I visited the famous Dresden gallery, unexcelled in the world. Its masterpieces are so well known that I render no special account. I will only observe that here, as everywhere else, one recognises how far Raphael stands above all other painters. I had inspected several rooms of the gallery, when I found myself before a picture which filled me with an admiration greater than anything else in the art of painting could have evoked. It represents the Virgin, standing on some clouds and holding the infant Jesus in her arms. This figure is of a beauty and a nobility worthy of the divine brush that traced it; the face of the child bears an expression at once innocent and heavenly; the draperies are most accurately drawn, and their colouring is exquisite. At the right of the Virgin is a saint done with admirable fidelity to life, his two hands being especially to be noted. At the left is a young saint, with head inclined, looking at two angels at the bottom of the picture. Her face is all loveliness, truth and modesty. The two little angels are leaning on their hands, their eyes raised to the persons above them, and their heads are done with an ingenuity and a delicacy not to be conveyed in words.

Being in great haste to get to St. Petersburg, I went

from Dresden to Berlin, where I only remained five days, my project being to return thither and make a longer stay on my way back from Russia, for the purpose of seeing Prussia's charming Queen.

CHAPTER VII

Saint Petersburg

ARRIVAL AT ST. PETERSBURG — THE BEAUTIFUL GRAND-DUCHESS ELISABETH — CATHERINE II. RECEIVES MME. LEBRUN — AND IS MOST GRACIOUS — PETTY COURT INTRIGUES — A VISIT TO COUNT STROGONOFF — HOSPITALITY OF THE RUSSIANS — AN AMBASSADOR AS GARDENER — PRINCESS DOLGORUKI AND HER HIDEOUS ADMIRER — THE EXTRAVAGANCES OF POTEMKIN — HIS END.

I ENTERED St. Petersburg on the 25th of July, 1795, by the road from Peterhoff, which gave me a favourable idea of the city, for this road is lined on both sides by delightful country houses, with gardens of the best taste in the English style. Their residents have taken advantage of the soil, which is very marshy, to adorn the gardens—where there are kiosks and pretty bridges—by canals and little streams. But it is a pity that a dreadful dampness spoils this pleasant scene of an evening; even before sunset such a fog rises over the road that one seems to be enveloped in thick, dark smoke.

Magnificent as I had conceived the city to be, I was enchanted by the aspect of its monuments, its handsome mansions, and its broad streets, one of which, called the Prospekt, is a mile long. The Neva, clear and limpid, cuts through the town, laden with vessels and barks unceasingly moving up and down, and this greatly adds to the liveliness of the town. The quays of the Neva are of granite, like those of the large canals dug through the town by Catherine.   On one bank of the river are splendid edifices: the Academy of Arts, the Academy of Sciences and a number of others are reflected in the Neva.   There was no grander sight on a moonlight night, I was told, than the bulk of those majestic piles, resembling ancient temples.   Altogether, St. Petersburg took me back to the times of Agamemnon, partly through the grandeur of the buildings and partly through the popular garb, which reminded me of the dress of antiquity.

Though I have just spoken of moonlight, I was unable to enjoy it at the time of my arrival, for in the month of July there is not a single hour of actual darkness in St. Petersburg.   The sun sets at about half-past ten, and it is merely dusk until twilight, which begins half an hour after midnight, so that one can always see plainly.   I have often supped at eleven o'clock by daylight.

My first care was to take a good rest, for, after Riga, the roads had been most horrible.   Large stones, one on top of the other, gave my carriage, which was one of the roughest in the world, a violent shock at every moment. And the inns being so bad as to exclude every possibility of staying at them, we had jolted and jerked on to St. Petersburg without a stop.

I was far from recovered from all my fatigue—since the term of my residence in St. Petersburg had been only twenty-four hours—when a visitor was announced in the person of the French Ambassador, Count Esterhazy.   He congratulated me on my arrival at St. Petersburg, telling me that he was about to inform the Empress of it and at the same time to take her orders for my presentation. Very little later I received a visit from the Count de Choiseul-Gouffier.   While conversing with him I confessed what happiness it would give me to see the great Catherine, but I did not dissemble the fright and embarrassment I expected to undergo when I should be presented to that powerful Princess. "You will find it quite easy," he replied. "When you see the Empress you will be surprised at her good nature; she is really an excellent woman." I acknowledge that I was astonished by his remark, the justice of which I could scarcely believe, in view of what I had heard up to that time. It is true that the Prince de Ligne, during the charming narration of his journey in the Crimea, had recounted several facts proving that this great Princess had manners that were as gracious as they were simple, but an excellent woman was hardly the thing to call her.

However, the same evening Count Esterhazy, on returning from Czarskoiesielo, where the Empress was living, came to tell me that Her Majesty would receive me the next day at one o'clock. Such a quick presentation, which I had not hoped for, put me into a very awkward position. I had nothing but very plain muslin dresses, as I usually wore no others, and it was impossible to have an ornamental gown made from one day to the next, even at St. Petersburg. Count Esterhazy had said he would call for me at ten o'clock precisely and take me to breakfast with his wife, who also lived at Czarskoiesielo, so that when the appointed hour struck I started with serious apprehensions about my dress, which certainly was no court dress. On arriving at Mme. d'Esterhazy's, I, in fact, took note of her amazement. Her obliging civility did not prevent her from asking me, "Have you not brought another gown?" I turned crimson at her question, and explained how time had been wanting to have a more suitable gown made. Her displeased looks increased my anxiety to such a degree that I needed to summon up all my courage when the moment came to go before the Empress.

The Count gave me his arm, and we were walking across a portion of the park, when, at a ground-floor window, I espied a young person who was watering a pot of pansies.

She was seventeen years old at most; her features were well formed and regular, her face a perfect oval; her fine complexion was not bright, but was of a paleness completely in harmony with the expression of her countenance, whose sweetness was angelic. Her fair hair floated over her neck and forehead. She was clad in a white tunic, a carelessly knotted girdle surrounding a waist as slender and supple as a nymph's. As I have described her, so ravishingly did this young person stand out against the background of her apartment, adorned with pillars and draped in pink and silver gauze, that I exclaimed, "That is Psyche!" It was Princess Elisabeth, the wife of Alexander. She addressed me, and kept me long enough to tell me a thousand flattering things. She then added, "We have wanted you here for a long time, Mme. Lebrun —so much so that I have sometimes dreamed you had already come." I parted from her with regret, and have always preserved a memory of that charming vision.

A few minutes later I was alone with the autocrat of all the Russias. The Ambassador had told me I must kiss her hand, in accordance with which custom she drew off one of her gloves, and this ought to have reminded me what to do. But I forgot all about it. The truth is, that the sight of this famous woman made such an impression upon me that I could not possibly think of anything else but to look at her. I was at first extremely surprised to find her short; I had imagined her a great height—something like her renown. She was very stout, but still had a handsome face, which her white hair framed to perfection. Genius seemed to have its seat on her broad, high forehead. Her eyes were soft and small, her nose was quite Greek, her complexion lively, and her features very mobile. She at once said in a voice that was soft though rather thick: "I am delighted, madame, to see you here; your reputation had preceded you. I am fond of the arts and especially of painting. I am not an adept, but a fancier."

Everything else she said during this interview, which was rather long, in reference to her wish that I might like Russia well enough to remain a long time, bore the stamp of such great amiability that my shyness vanished, and by the time I took leave of Her Majesty I was entirely reassured. Only I could not forgive myself for not having kissed her hand, which was very beautiful and very white, and I deplored that oversight the more as Count Esterhazy reproached me with it. As for what I was wearing, she did not seem to have paid the least attention to it. Or else perhaps she may have been easier to please than our Ambassadress.

I went over part of the gardens at Czarskoiesielo, which are a veritable little fairyland. The Empress had a terrace from them communicating with her apartment, and on this terrace she kept a large number of birds. I was told that every morning she went out to feed them, and that this was one of her chief pleasures.

Directly after my audience Her Majesty testified her wish to have me spend the summer in that beautiful region. She commanded her stewards, of whom the old Prince Bariatinski was one, to give me an apartment in the castle, as she desired to have me near her, so that she might see me paint. But I afterward found out that these gentlemen took no pains to put me near the Empress, and that in spite of her repeated orders they always maintained that they had no lodgings at their disposal. What astonished me most of all, when I was informed of this matter, was that these courtiers, suspecting me to belong to the party of the Count d'Artois, were afraid lest I had come to get Esterhazy replaced by another Ambassador. It is probable that the Count was in connivance with them about all this, but anybody was surely little acquainted with me who did not know that I was too busy with my art to give any time to politics, even if I had not always felt an aversion to everything smacking of intrigue.

Moreover, aside from the honour of being lodged with the Empress and the pleasure of inhabiting such a fine place, everything would have been stiff and irksome for me at Czarskoiesielo. I have always had the greatest need to enjoy my liberty, and, for the sake of following my own inclination, I have always infinitely preferred living in my own house.

Moreover, the reception I met with in Russia was well calculated to console me for a petty court intrigue. I cannot say how eagerly and with what kind-hearted affability a stranger is sought after in this country, especially if possessing some talent. My letters of introduction became quite superfluous; not only was I at once invited to live with the best and pleasantest families, but I found several former acquaintances in St. Petersburg, and even some old friends. First, there was Count Strogonoff, a true lover of the arts, whose portrait I had painted at Paris in my early youth. It was to us both an extreme pleasure to meet once more. He owned a splendid collection of pictures in St. Petersburg, and near the town, at Kaminostroff, a delightful Italian villa, where he gave a great dinner every Sunday. He called for me to take me there, and I was enraptured with the place. The villa stood by the high road, and its windows overlooked the Neva. The garden, whose boundaries were immense, was laid out in the English manner. A number of boats arrived from all directions, bringing visitors to Count Strogonoff's, for a number of people who were not invited to dinner came to walk in the park. The Count also allowed merchants to set up their stalls there, so that this beautiful place was enlivened with an amusing fair, especially as the costumes of the different neighbouring districts were picturesque and varied.

About three o'clock we went up on a covered terrace lined with pillars, bright daylight falling between them from every side. On one hand we enjoyed the view of the park, and on the other that of the Neva, covered with a thousand boats. The weather was the finest in the world, for the summers are splendid in Russia, a country that in July I have often found hotter than Italy. We dined on this same terrace, and the dinner was magnificent; at dessert gorgeous fruits were served, and remarkably fine melons, which seemed to me a great luxury. As soon as we sat down at table delightful instrumental music was heard, and continued throughout the dinner. The overture to "Iphigenia" was executed entrancingly. I was greatly surprised when Count Strogonoff informed me that each of the musicians played but one note; it was impossible for me to conceive how all these individual sounds could form into such a perfect whole, and how any expression could grow out of such a mechanical performance.

After dinner we took a delightful walk in the park; then, toward evening, we went back to the terrace, whence, at nightfall, we witnessed a very fine display of fireworks which the Count had had in store for us. Reflected in the waters of the Neva, these fireworks were of beautiful effect. Finally, by way of concluding the pleasures of the day, there arrived in two very narrow little boats some Indians, who danced before us. Their dances consisted in going through light movements without stirring from their places, and entertained us considerably.

Count Strogonoff's house was far from being the only one kept with such splendour. At St. Petersburg, as at Moscow, a number of noblemen owning enormous fortunes were in the habit of setting an open table, so that a well-recommended stranger was never under the necessity of having recourse to an inn. There was a dinner or a supper everywhere; nothing was embarrassing but your choice. I remember, toward the end of my stay in St. Petersburg, how Prince Narischkin,

the Grand Equerry, always held open table to the extent
of twenty-five or thirty covers for strangers who were
recommended to him. These hospitable customs exist
in the interior of Russia, whither modern civilisation
has not yet penetrated. When Russian noblemen
go upon visits to their estates, which are usually situated
at great distances from the capital, they stop on the
way in the houses of their countrymen, where, without
being personally known by the host, they, their servants
and their horses are taken in and treated as handsomely
as possible, even should they remain a month.

I once saw a traveller who had journeyed across
this vast country with two friends. All three
had traversed those distant provinces as they might
have done during the Golden Age, in the days of
the patriarchs. They had everywhere been lodged
and fed with such liberality that their purses had
become almost useless. They had not been able to
so much as force drink-money on the people who
had waited upon them and cared for their horses.
Their hosts, who for the most part were traders or
husbandmen, had expressed astonishment at the
warmth of their gratitude. "If we were in your
country," said they, "you would do the same for
us." I only wish this had been true.

The summer ends in Russia with the month of August,
and there is no autumn. I often went walking at
Czarskoiesielo, whose park, bounded by the sea, is one
of the loveliest sights imaginable. It is full of monuments which the Empress was wont to call her caprices.
There are a superb marble bridge in the Palladian style,
Turkish baths—trophies of Romazoff's and Orloff's
victories—a temple with thirty-two pillars, and then
the colonnade and the great stairway of Hercules. The
park has unrivalled avenues of trees. Opposite the
castle is a long, broad lawn, and at the end of it a

cherry orchard, where I remember having frequently eaten excellent cherries.

Count Cobentzel very much wished me to make the acquaintance of a woman whose cleverness and beauty I had often heard vaunted—the Princess Dolgoruki. I received an invitation from her to dine at Alexandrovski, where she had a country house, and the Count came for me to take me there with my daughter. This very large house was furnished without ostentation, and it was a great pleasure to me to watch the continual passage of the boats, in which the rowers sang in chorus. The songs of the Russian people have a somewhat barbarous originality, but are melancholy and melodious.

The beauty of Princess Dolgoruki struck me very much. Her features had the Greek character mixed with something Jewish, especially in profile. Her long, dark chestnut hair, carelessly taken up, touched her shoulders. Her figure was perfect, and in her whole person she exhibited at once nobility and grace without the least affectation. She received me with so much amiability and civility that I willingly acceded to her request that I might stay a week with her. The charming Princess Kurakin, whose acquaintance I had made, was living with the Princess Dolgoruki, these ladies and Count Cobentzel keeping house together. The company was very numerous, and no one thought of anything but amusement. After dinner we took delightful rides in handsome boats furnished with red velvet, gold-fringed curtains. A choir, preceding us in a plainer boat, charmed us with their singing, which was always perfectly exact, even at the highest notes. The day of my arrival we had music in the evening; the next day there was a delightful play. Dalayrac's "Underground" was given. Princess Dolgoruki played the part of Camille; young De la Ribaussière, who afterward became minister in Russia, played the boy; and Count

Cobentzel, the gardener. I remember how, during the performance, a messenger arrived from Vienna with despatches for the Count, who was Austrian Ambassador at St. Petersburg, and how, at the sight of the man dressed as a gardener, he did not want to give up the despatches, this giving rise to a most diverting argument between them behind the scenes. At the end of the week, the whole of which had seemed to last but a minute, I was obliged, to my regret, to leave the hospitable roof of Princess Dolgoruki, as I had made a number of engagements to paint portraits. I, however, formed several connections at Alexandrovski which proved infinitely agreeable during my whole stay in Russia.

Count Cobentzel was passionately devoted to the Princess Dolgoruki, without her responding in the least to his importunities; but the coolness she showed toward his intentions by no means drove him away. His sole object was the happiness of being in her presence; whether in the country or in town, he scarcely ever left her for a moment. So soon as his despatches, written with great facility, were sent off, he rushed to her side and made a complete slave of himself. He was seen to fly at the least word, the least gesture of his divinity. If a play was given he took any part she offered him, even if the rôle was not at all suited to his appearance. For Count Cobentzel, who looked about fifty, was very ugly, and squinted horribly. He was rather tall, but also extremely fat, which, however, did not prevent him from being quite active, particularly when it was a case of executing the demands of his dearly beloved Princess. Otherwise he was quick and clever, his conversation was enlivened with a thousand anecdotes which he could recount to perfection, and I always knew him as the best and most obliging of men.

What made the Princess Dolgoruki indifferent to the

sighs of Count Cobentzel and to those of many other
admirers was the fact that from one of them she had
received attentions more brilliant than ever woman
had had lavished upon her by any lovelorn king. The
famous Potemkin—he who had said the word "impossible"
should be ruled out of the dictionary—had testified his
adoration for her with a magnificence surpassing all that
we read of in the "Thousand and One Nights." When,
in 1791, after making her journey in the Crimea, the
Empress Catherine II. returned to St. Petersburg, Prince
Potemkin remained behind in command of the army,
several of the generals having brought their wives.
It was then that he had occasion to meet Princess
Dolgoruki. Her name, too, was Catherine, and the
Prince made a great banquet for her, nominally in
honour of the Empress. At table the Princess was seated
by his side. At dessert, on the table were put crystal
goblets full of diamonds, which were served to the ladies
by the spoonful. The queen of the festival observing
this luxury, Potemkin whispered to her, "Since this
celebration is for you, why should you be astonished
at anything?" He would spare no sacrifice to satisfy
a wish or a whim of that charming woman. Learning
one day that she was in want of ball slippers of a kind
she usually sent for to France, Potemkin despatched
an express messenger to Paris, who hastened day and
night to bring back these slippers. It was well known
in St. Petersburg that to afford the Princess Dolgoruki
a spectacle he much desired her to see he had assaulted
the fortress of Otschakoff sooner than had been agreed
upon, and perhaps sooner than was prudent.

No woman, it seems so me, had greater dignity of
mien and manner than Princess Dolgoruki. Having
seen my "Sibyl," about which she was very enthusiastic,
she wished me to make her portrait in this style, and I
had the pleasure of doing her bidding to her entire

satisfaction. The portrait done, she sent me a very handsome carriage, and put on my arm a bracelet made of a tress of her hair with a diamond inscription reading, "Adorn her who adorns her century." I was deeply touched by the graciousness and delicacy of such a gift.

At the time of my reaching St. Petersburg, Prince Potemkin had already been there some years, but he was still spoken of as though he had been a wizard. Some idea of what an extraordinary and high-flying imagination he had may be obtained from reading what the Prince de Ligne and the Count de Ségur have written about the journey he arranged for the Empress Catherine II. in the Crimea; those palaces, those wooden villages built all along the route, as if by a magic wand, that huge forest going up in flames by way of fireworks for Her Majesty—the whole journey, in fact, was a fantastic affair. His niece, Countess Skavronska, said to me in Vienna, "Had my uncle known you, he would have loaded you with distinctions and riches." Certain it is that at every opportunity this famous man was generous to prodigality and luxurious to madness. All his tastes were extravagant, all his habits royal, so much so that, although he possessed a fortune exceeding that of some sovereigns, the Prince de Ligne told me that he had known him to be without money.

Favour and power had accustomed Prince Potemkin to satisfy his slightest desires. Here is an example which proves the point. One day, when the talk ran on the size of one of his adjutants, he declared that a certain officer in the Russian army—whom he named—was taller still. After every one who knew the officer in question had contradicted Potemkin, he forthwith sent off a messenger with an order to bring back with him this officer, who was then eight hundred miles away. Upon hearing that he had been sent for by the Prince, his joy was unbounded, since he believed that he had been promoted to a higher rank. His disappointment may therefore be imagined when, on his arrival in camp, he was informed that he was to be measured with Potemkin's adjutant, and that he must then return without any other reward than the fatigue of the long journey.

The man whom a long period of favour had, so to say, accustomed to reign beside the sovereign was unable to survive the thought of disgrace. Catherine II. sent to Prince Repnin her orders to treat for peace, to which Potemkin was strongly opposed. Angry as possible, he set out upon the instant in the hope of preventing the signature, but only to learn at Yassy that peace was concluded. This news was fatal to him. Already indisposed, he now fell mortally ill, which did not hinder him from at once beginning the return journey to St. Petersburg. But in a few hours his ailment grew so serious that it became out of the question for him to support the movement of a carriage. He was laid out in a meadow and covered with his cloak, and there Potemkin breathed his last sigh, on the 15th of October, 1791, in the arms of Countess Branicka, his niece. Plato Zouboff, a young lieutenant of the guard, succeeded Potemkin in the favour of the Empress, who showered honours and wealth upon him.

CHAPTER VIII

LIFE IN RUSSIA

PAINTING RUSSIAN ROYALTIES — FESTIVITIES AT COURT — THE PANGS OF WAITING FOR DINNER — "TO KEEP WARM, SPEND THE WINTER IN RUSSIA" — THE HARDINESS OF ITS COMMON PEOPLE — WHO ARE WELL SUITED WITH SERFDOM — AND REMARKABLY HONEST — THE QUAINT CEREMONIAL OF BLESSING THE NEVA — VARIOUS SOCIAL CUSTOMS.

UPON Her Majesty's return from Czarskoiesielo Count Strogonoff came to me with her command to paint the two Grand Duchesses, Alexandrina and Helen. These Princesses might have been thirteen or fourteen years old, and their faces were angelic, though of entirely different expression. Their complexions especially were so tender and delicate that one might have supposed they lived on ambrosia. The eldest, Alexandrina, was of the Greek type of beauty, and very much resembled Alexander, but the face of the younger, Helen, was far more subtle. I grouped them together, holding and looking at the Empress's portrait; their dress was somewhat Greek in style, quite simple and modest. As soon as I had done their pictures the Empress ordered me to paint the Grand Duchess Elisabeth, not long married to Alexander. I have already said what a ravishing person this Princess was; I should very much have liked not to represent such a heavenly figure in common dress, and I have always wanted to paint an historical picture of her and Alexander,

96

so regular were the features of both. I painted her standing, in full court dress, arranging some flowers near a basketful of others. When I had done her large portrait she had another done for her mother, in which I painted her leaning on a cushion, with a diaphanous violet wrap. I can say that the more sittings the Grand Duchess Elisabeth gave me, the kinder and more affectionate did she become. One morning, while she was posing, I was seized with a giddy fit and grew so dazed that I had to close my eyes. She took alarm, and herself quickly ran for water, bathed my eyes, tended me with inexpressible kindness, and sent to inquire after me as soon as I had got home. About this time, too, I did a portrait of the Grand Duchess Anne, the wife of the Grand Duke Constantine. She, born as Princess of Coburg, without having a celestial face like her sister-in-law, was nevertheless sweetly pretty. She was probably sixteen, and her features were all life and mirth. Not that this young Princess ever knew much happiness in Russia. If it can be said that Alexander inherited his good looks and his character from his mother, it is equally true that this was not the case with Constantine, who strongly resembled his father, without, however, being quite as ugly, but like him endowed with a marvellously quick temper.

In that era the Russian court usually included such a large number of beautiful women that a ball at the Empress afforded an exquisite sight. I was present at the most magnificent ball she ever gave. The Empress, grandly arrayed, sat at the end of the room, attended by the first personages of the court. Close to her stood the Grand Duchess Marie, and Paul, Alexander and Constantine. An open balustrade separated them from the space where the dancing was going forward. The ball consisted of nothing but repetitions of the dance called "polonaise," in which I had for my first partner young

Prince Bariatinski, with whom I went the round of the
room and afterward took a seat on the bench to watch
all the dancers.   I could not tell how many pretty women
I saw pass before me, but I cannot help saying that,
amidst all these beauties, the Princesses of the imperial
family carried off the palm.   They were all habited in
Greek costumes, with tunics attached at the shoulder
with large diamond buckles.   I had taken a hand in the
Grand Duchess Elisabeth's dress, so that her costume
was the most correct.   Paul's daughters, however, Helen
and Alexandrina, wore on their heads veils of light-blue
gauze, strewn with silver, which lent their faces an almost
divine appearance.   The splendour of all that surrounded
the Empress, the gorgeousness of the room, the handsome
people, the profusion of diamonds, and the sparkling of
the thousand lights made a veritable enchantment of
this ball.

A few days later I went to a gala dinner at court.
When I entered the room the invited ladies were all there,
standing by the table, on which the first dish was already
served.   A moment after, a large door with two valves
was thrown open, and the Empress appeared.   I have said
that she was short, but nevertheless on state occasions,
her erect head, her eagle eye, her countenance so used to
command—all was so symbolic of majesty that she seemed
to be the queen of the world.   She wore the ribbons of
three orders.   Her garb was plain and dignified, con-
sisting of a muslin tunic embroidered with gold and
enclasped by a diamond belt, a pair of wide sleeves being
turned back in oriental fashion.   Over this tunic was a
red velvet dolman with very short sleeves.   The cap
set on her white hair was not adorned with bows, but
with diamonds of the greatest beauty.   When Her
Majesty had taken her place all the ladies sat down to the
table, and, according to universal custom, laid their napkins on their knees, while the Empress fastened hers with

two pins, just as napkins are fastened on children. She soon noticed that the ladies did not eat, and suddenly burst out: "Ladies, you do not want to follow my example, and you are only pretending to eat! I have adopted the habit of pinning my napkin, as otherwise I could not even eat an egg without spilling some of it on my collar."

I, in fact, observed her to dine with a very hearty appetite. A good orchestra played during the whole meal, the musicians being in a large gallery at the end of the room.

Relating to dinners, I may say here that certainly the saddest I ever went to at St. Petersburg was at a sister's of Zuboff, where I had neglected to present a letter of introduction. Six months of my sojourn in Russia had gone by, when I met her one evening coming out of the theatre. She stepped over to me and said most politely that she was still waiting for a letter which had been given to me for her. Scarcely knowing what excuse to make, I replied that I had mislaid the letter, but that I would look for it again and hasten to bring it to her. I accordingly went one morning to visit the Countess D——, and she invited me to dine with her the day after the next. It was then the custom all over St. Petersburg to dine at half-past two, and I therefore went to the Countess's at that hour with my daughter, who was also invited. We were conducted to a very melancholy drawing-room, on the way to which I observed no preparations whatever for dinner. One hour, two hours went by, but there was no more question of sitting down to table than if we had just taken our morning coffee. At last two servants came in and opened several card-tables, and although it seemed rather strange to me that any one should eat in a drawing-room, I flattered myself that dinner was now to be served. But I was wrong. The servants went out, and in a few minutes a number

of the guests had settled down to play cards. About
six o'clock my poor daughter and I were so starved that,
when we looked into a mirror, we were frightened and
sorry for ourselves. I felt as if I should die. Not until
half-past seven were we informed that the meal was
ready; but our poor stomachs had gone through too much
agony; we were unable to eat anything at all. I then
found out that the Countess D—— dined at the hour
usual in London. The Countess ought to have notified
me, but perhaps she imagined that the whole universe
was aware of her dinner hour.

As a rule, nothing was more distasteful to me than to
dine in town, but I was sometimes obliged to do it, especially in Russia, where one runs a risk of mortally offend-
ing people if one declines their invitations too often.   I
disliked the dinners the more as there were such a number
of them. They were highly luxurious; most of the
nobility had very good French cooks, and the fare was
incomparable. A quarter of an hour before the guests
sat down at table a servant would pass round a tray
with all sorts of cordials and small slices of buttered
bread. No cordials were taken after dinner, but always
superior Malaga wine.

It is the custom in Russia for the great ladies, even at
their own houses, to go into table before the guests, so
that the Princess Dolgoruki and others would take me
by the arm, in order that I might go in at the same time
as they, for it would be impossible to exceed the Russian
ladies in the urbanities of good society. I will even
go so far as to say that they are without the haughtiness
chargeable to some of our French ladies.

At St. Petersburg the rigour of the climate would be
unnoticed by any one who remains indoors, to such a
degree have the Russians perfected the means of keeping
their houses warm. From the very porter's door all is
heated by such excellent stoves that the fires main-

tained in the chimney places are purely ornamental. The stairways and corridors are of the same temperature as the rooms, whose communicating doors are left open without any inconvenience resulting. When the Emperor Paul, then Grand Duke only, came to France for the first time, he said to the Parisians: "In St. Petersburg you see the cold, but here you feel it." And when, after spending seven and a half years in Russia, I went back to Paris, where the Princess Dolgoruki was also staying, I remember that on a certain day, on which I had gone to see her, we were both so cold in front of her fireplace that we said, "We must go to spend the winter in Russia to get warm."

For going out, such precautions are taken that even foreigners are hardly affected by the severity of the weather. Every one wears velvet, fur-lined boots in his carriage, and cloaks likewise heavily lined with fur. At seventeen degrees below zero the theatres are closed, and every one remains at home. I am perhaps the only person who, not suspecting how cold it was, ever took it into my head to pay a visit when the thermometer was at eighteen. The Countess Golovin lived rather far away, in the broad street called the Prospekt, and from my house to hers I met not a single carriage, which surprised me considerably. I nevertheless went on. The cold was such that at first I thought my carriage windows must be open. Upon seeing me enter her drawing-room, the Countess exclaimed: "Heavens! How could you go out this evening? Do you not know that it is nearly twenty degrees?" This made me think of my poor coachman, and without taking off my pelisse I at once returned to my carriage, and was driven home as quickly as possible. But the cold had so attacked my head that I was benumbed. My head was treated with Cologne water to restore the circulation; otherwise I should have gone mad.

One very astonishing thing is the small effect which
this severe temperature has on the common people. Far
from their health suffering in consequence, it has been
observed that there are more centenarians in Russia
than anywhere else. In St. Petersburg, as in Moscow,
the great lords and all the notables of the empire drive
six- or eight-in-hand; their postilions are little boys of
eight or ten, who ride with amazing dexterity. There
are from two to eight horses, and it is curious how these
little fellows, so lightly clad, with their shirts sometimes
open on their chests, cheerfully expose themselves to
cold which certainly would kill a French or Prussian
grenadier in a few hours. As for me, who was content
with two horses for my carriage, I was surprised at the
submissiveness and resignation of the coachmen. They
never complained. In the most rigorous weather, when
waiting for their masters either at the theatre or
a ball, they sit still without budging, and only knock
their feet against the box to get a little warmth, while
the little postilions lie down at the bottom of the stair-
cases. I must acknowledge, however, that the coachmen are provided by their masters with furred coats and
gloves, and that, in the event of the cold being unusual,
if any noblemen gives a party or a ball he has strong
liquor distributed among them, and wood to build camp-
fires in the courtyard and the street.

The common people of Russia are in general ugly,
but their behaviour is at once simple and dignified, and
they are the best creatures in the world. One never
sees a drunken man, although the popular beverage is
corn brandy. Most of the Russians of this class live on
potatoes and garlic, with oil, which they eat with their
bread, so that they always stink, although it is their
habit to take a bath every Saturday. But their food
does not prevent them from singing loudly when at work
or rowing their boats, and they often reminded me of

something the Marquis de Chastellux said one evening at my house about the beginning of the Revolution: "If their bonds are taken off they will be much more unhappy!"

The Russians are clever and capable, since they learn all trades with great ease, some of them even gaining success in the arts. One day, at Count Strogonoff's, I saw an architect who had once been his serf. This young man exhibited so much talent that the Count made a present of him to the Emperor Paul, who made him one of his architects and ordered him to build a theatre-hall after the plans designed and submitted by him. I never saw the hall, but was told that it was very handsome. In the matter of artistic serfs I was less fortunate than the Count. As I found myself without a man-servant, after being robbed by one I had brought from Vienna, Count Strogonoff gave me one of his serfs, who was supposed to prepare his daughter-in-law's palette and clean her brushes when she amused herself with painting. This youth, whom I therefore engaged for the same purpose, became persuaded, after serving me for a fortnight, that he was a painter, too, and gave me no rest until I had obtained his freedom from the Count to enable him to work with the Academy students. He wrote me some letters on this subject that were really curiosities of style and ideas. The Count, in yielding to my request, had said, "You may be sure that before long he will want to come back." I gave the young man twenty rubles and the Count gave him at least as much. Accordingly, he at once hastened to purchase the uniform of the students in painting, and thus attired came to thank me with a triumphant air. About two months later he brought me a large family picture, which was so bad that I could not look at it, and for which the poor young man had been paid so little that, after liquidating all his expenses, he had lost eight rubles of his money. As the Count had

foreseen, his disappointment made him surrender his
wretched liberty and go back to his master.

The servants are remarkable for their intelligence. I
had one who knew not a word of French, and although
I was equally ignorant of Russian we understood each
other perfectly without the agency of speech. By raising
my arm I asked him for my easel, or my paint box, or
otherwise conveyed to him by gesture what articles I
wanted. He invariably seized my meaning, and was
of the greatest value to me. Another very precious
quality I discovered in him was his honesty, which was
proof against all temptations. Frequently bank-notes
were remitted to me in payment of my pictures, and
when I was busy painting I laid them near me on a table.
On quitting work I constantly forgot to take away the
notes, which sometimes lay there three or four days
without his ever abstracting one. Moreover, he was
a man of exceptional sobriety; I never once saw him
drunk. This good servant was called Peter; he wept
when I left St. Petersburg, and I have always sincerely
regretted losing him.

The Russian people in general are honest and gentle
by nature. At St. Petersburg or Moscow not only are
great crimes never heard of, but one never hears of thefts.
This good and quiet behaviour, surprising in men little
beyond barbarism, is attributed by many to the system
of servitude they are under. As for me, I believe the
reason to be that the Russians are extremely religious.

Not long after my arrival at St. Petersburg I went into
the country to see the daughter-in-law of my old friend,
Count Strogonoff. His house at Kaminostroff was situated at the right of the great highway skirting the Neva.
I alighted from my carriage, opened a little wicket giving
admission to the garden, and reached a room on the
ground floor whose door was wide open. So it was very
easy to enter Countess Strogonoff's house. Consequently,

when I found her in a little sitting-room, and she showed
me her apartments, I was greatly astonished to see all
her jewels near a window looking out on the garden and
therefore within close reach of the high road. This seemed
to me the more imprudent as Russian ladies are in the
habit of exhibiting their diamonds and other ornaments
under large cases, such as are to be seen in jewellers'
shops. "Countess," I asked her, "are you not afraid
of being robbed?" "No," was her answer; "there are the
best police." And she pointed out, above the jewel-box,
various images of the Virgin, and St. Nicholas, the patron
saint of the country, with a lamp burning in front of them.
It is a fact that, during the seven years and more which
I spent in Russia, I on all occasions observed the image
of the Virgin, or of a saint, and the presence of a child,
to have something sacred for a Russian.

The common people, in speaking to you, never address
you otherwise, according to your age, than as mother,
father, brother or sister, and in this usage every one is
included, even the Emperor and the Empress and the
whole imperial family. In the class above the populace
there are a number of people in comfortable circumstances
and others very well-to-do. The tradesmen's wives, for
instance, spend a great deal on dress, without this appear-
ing to impose any restriction on household expenses.
Their head-dress especially is always fine and fashionable.
On their caps, whose flaps are usually embroidered with
small pearls, they wear a broad piece of stuff which falls
from the head to the shoulders and down the whole
back. This sort of veil throws a shadow on the face,
which they assuredly need, seeing that all of them, I know
not why, whiten and rouge their faces and pencil their
eyebrows in the most absurd manner.

When the month of May comes to St. Petersburg
there is no evidence of spring flowers embalming the air,
nor of the nightingale's song, celebrated so much by the

poets. The ground is covered with half-melted snow. The Doga brings into the Neva ice blocks as large as enormous rocks, heaped on top of each other, and these ice blocks renew the cold which has diminished with the breaking of the Neva. This dissolution might be called a splendid horror; the noise of it is fearful. Close to the exchange the Neva is three times as wide as the Seine at the Pont Royal, and one may imagine the effect of this sea of ice cracking in all its parts. In spite of the officials posted all along the quays to prohibit the people from jumping from floe to floe, the boldest venture upon the moving ice for the purpose of crossing the river. Before undertaking their dangerous expedition they make the sign of the cross, and then rush on, fully persuaded that if they perish it must be because they were predestined to it. The first who crosses the Neva in a boat at the hour of the breaking up presents a silver cup, full of river water, to the Emperor, who in turn fills it with gold.

The windows are still left stuffed up at this season. Russia has no spring, but the vegetation hastens to make up for lost time. One may say with literal truth that the leaves sprout while you watch them. One day at the end of May I went with my daughter for a walk in the Summer Garden, and, wishing to assure ourselves as to the truth of all we had heard concerning the rapidity of vegetable growth, we took note of some shrub-leaves that were only in bud. We took a long turn in the avenue, then coming back to the spot we had started from, we found the buds open and the leaves completely unrolled.

The Russians take advantage of all phases of their climate to enjoy themselves. In the severest cold they indulge in sledging parties, either by day or with torches at night. In some places they throw up mountains of snow, down which they slide at a stupendous rate of speed without any danger. Men versed in their business

1. The Artist's Brother, Louis Jean Baptiste Etienne
Vigée (born Paris, 1758–died Paris, 1820), 1773. The Saint
Louis Art Museum, Museum Purchase.

2. The Artist's reception piece to the Academy: "Peace Bringing Back Abundance," 1780. The Louvre, Paris.

3. Portrait of Madame Etienne Vigée, neé Suzanne Marie
Françoise Rivière, 1785. Private collection, New York.
Courtesy Wildenstein & Co., Inc.

4. Sleeping Child (study for the Artist's masterpiece, the large dynastic portrait of Marie Antoinette and her Children), 1786. Private collection. Courtesy Wildenstein & Co., Inc.

5.   Portrait of Emmanual de Crussol, 1787. The
Metropolitan Museum of Art, The Jules Bache Collection,
1949. (49.7.53)

6.   Portrait of the Artist, Hubert Robert, 1788.
The Louvre, Paris.

7.   Portrait of Otto Nicholas, Prince of Nassau-Sieghen,
1789. Private collection, New York. Courtesy
Wildenstein & Co., Inc.

8. Self-Portrait of the Artist in Pastel, c. 1790. Private collection, U.S.A. Courtesy Wildenstein & Co., Inc.

push you off from the top of the mountain, and others catch you at the bottom.

One of the most interesting ceremonies to be seen is the blessing of the Neva. It occurs once a year, and it is the Archimandrite who bestows the benediction in presence of the Emperor, the imperial family, and all the dignitaries. As at this season the ice of the Neva is at least three feet thick, a hole is made through which, after the ceremony, everybody draws up some of the holy water. Frequently women are seen to dip their little children in, and sometimes the unfortunate mothers let loose their hold of the poor victims of superstition. But instead of mourning the loss of her child, the mother then gives thanks for the happiness of the angel who has gone to pray for her. The Emperor is obliged to drink the first glass of water, it being tendered him by the Archimandrite.

I have already said that in St. Petersburg you must go out into the street to find out how cold it is. And it is likewise true that the Russians are not content with giving their houses a springlike temperature; some of their rooms are lined with windowed screens, behind which are arranged boxes and pots containing the lovely flowers that the month of May gives to France. In winter the rooms are lighted most elaborately. They are also scented with hot vinegar into which bits of mint have been thrown and which yields a very agreeable and healthy smell. All apartments are furnished with long, broad divans for men and women to sit on. I became so used to them that after a time I could not sit on a chair.

The Russian lady's salute is a bow, seeming to me more dignified and graceful than our courtesy. They do not ring for their servants, but signal to them by clapping their hands together, as sultanas are said to do in the harems. Every Russian lady has a man in full livery at the door of her drawing-room; he is always there to open the door for visitors, whom it was at that time the custom not to announce by name. But what seemed stranger still to me was that some of these ladies made a female serf sleep under their bed.

Of an evening I went out into society. There were innumerable balls, concerts and theatrical performances, and I thoroughly enjoyed these gatherings, where I found all the urbanity, all the grace of French company. It seemed as though good taste had made a jump with both feet from Paris to St. Petersburg. Nor was there a lack of open houses, and in all of them one was welcomed with the greatest hospitality. One met at about eight and supped at ten. In the meantime tea was drunk, like everywhere else. But the Russian tea is so excellent that I—with whom it does not agree, and who must abstain from it—was glad to inhale its aroma. Instead of tea I drank hydromel. This tasty beverage is made with good honey and a small fruit picked in the Russian woods; it is left in the cellar for a certain length of time before bottling. I found it far preferable to cider, beer, or even lemonade.

CHAPTER IX

CATHERINE II.

SURROUNDINGS OF ST. PETERSBURG — PATRIARCHAL UN-
CONVENTIONALITIES — AN ARTILLERY REPAST — THE
GREATNESS OF THE SECOND CATHERINE — WHO LIT
HER OWN FIRE AND MADE HER OWN COFFEE — AND
WAS SWORN AT BY A CHIMNEY SWEEPER — OTHER
DOMESTIC AMENITIES IN THE CAREER OF AN EMPRESS —
THE SUIT OF GUSTAVUS IV. — CATHERINE'S DEATH —
HUMILIATING FUNERAL INCIDENTS

I EXPERIENCED a great joy when, after breathing frosty
air outdoors and air heated by stoves indoors for several
months, I witnessed the arrival of summer. I took a
great delight in the walks, and hastened to enjoy the
beautiful surroundings of St. Petersburg. I very often
went to the Lake of Pergola alone with my Russian man-
servant to take what I called an air-bath. I enjoyed
the contemplation of its limpid water, which vividly
reflected the trees on its banks. And then I would
mount to the heights adjacent. On one side the horizon
was bounded by the sea and I could distinguish the
sails lit up by the sun. Here a silence reigned that was
disturbed only by the song of a thousand birds, or sometimes by the sound of a distant bell. The pure air and the
wild, picturesque place enchanted me. My faithful
Peter, who warmed up my little dinner or picked flowers
of the field for me, made me think of Robinson on his
island with Friday.

The heat being considerable, I often went with my

daughter for early walks on the island of Krestovski.
The extreme point of this island seemed to merge into
the sea, on which large vessels were navigating. Sometimes we went there in the evening to see the Russian
peasants dance, their national dress being very picturesque. I remember, on the subject of the excessive
heat often prevailing at St. Petersburg, a certain day
in the month of July of some year in which that month
was hotter than in Italy. On this day I saw Princess
Dolgoruki's mother, Princess Bariatinski, who was
once as lovely as an angel, and whose clever and spontaneous wit rendered her one of the most fascinating
women of St. Petersburg, established in her cellar,
with her lady's companion seated on the bottom step,
very quietly reading to her from a book.

But to return to the island of Krestovski. Taking
a row in a boat one day, we came upon a crowd of men
and women all bathing together. We even saw from a
distance young men naked on horseback, who were thus
bathing with their horses. In any other country one
would have been shocked by this, but the Russian
people are really primitively ingenuous. In the winter
husband, wife and children sleep together on the stove;
if the stove is not large enough, they lie on wooden
benches lining their hut, wrapped up simply in their
sheepskins. These good people have kept the customs of the ancient patriarchs.

A walk which pleased me particularly was one on
the island of Zelaguin, which, though it had once been
a very handsome garden, was now deserted. However,
there remained some lovely trees, charming avenues, a
temple surrounded with magnificent weeping willows,
flowers to please the eye, little running streams, and
bridges after the English fashion. In order to enjoy
this walk to the full, I took a little house opposite on the
bank of the Neva. The advantageous situation of my

cottage was combined with pleasing diversion, due to the fact that most of the boats, of which there was an unceasing procession up and down the river, gave me a continuous concert of vocal music or wind instruments.

The artillery general, Melissimo, lived in a pretty house close to mine, and I enjoyed having him for my neighbour, since he was the best and most obliging of men. As the General had spent much time in Turkey, his house was a model of Oriental comfort and luxury. There was a bathroom lighted from above, in the middle of which was a basin large enough to hold a dozen people. One went down into the water by steps. Linen to be used for drying the body after bathing was hung on a golden balustrade circling the basin, and consisted of large pieces of Indian mull worked at the bottom in flowers and gold, so that the weight of this embroidery caused the mull to adhere to the skin, which appeared to me an elaborate refinement. Round the room ran a broad divan on which one could stretch oneself and rest after taking a bath, and one of the doors opened from a sweet little sitting-room. This sitting-room, again, overlooked an odorous flower-bed, and some of the stems grew to the height of the window. It was in this room that the General gave us a breakfast of fruits, cream cheese and excellent Mocha coffee, on all of which my daughter regaled herself royally. Another time he asked us to a very good dinner, and had it served under a Turkish tent brought back from one of his journeys. The tent was put up on the lawn facing the house. There were twelve of us, all seated by the table on splendid divans. We were served with delicious fruits at dessert. The whole dinner was quite Asiatic, and the General's courtesy added to the savour of all the good things. I wish, however, that he had omitted firing off cannon shots in our immediate proximity just as we were sitting down at table, but

I was informed that such was the custom with all generals. I took my little house on the Neva for one summer only. The next, young Count Strogonoff lent me one at Kaminstroff, where I was very well suited. Every morning I walked alone in a neighbouring wood and passed my evenings with Countess Golovin, my neighbour. There I met young Prince Bariatinski, Princess Tarent, and various other congenial people. We would chat or have readings until supper time. In fact time was speeding by for me in the most agreeable manner.

The Russian people lived very happily under the rule of Catherine; by great and lowly have I heard the name of her blessed to whom the nation owed so much glory and so much well-being. I do not speak of the conquests by which the national vanity was so prodigiously flattered, but of the real, lasting good that this Empress did her people. During the space of the thirty-four years she reigned, her beneficent genius fathered or furthered all that was useful, all that was grand. She erected an immortal monument to Peter I.; she built two hundred and thirty-seven towns in stone, saying that wooden villages cost much more because they burned down so often; she covered the sea with her fleets; she established everywhere manufactories and banks, highly propitious to the commerce of St. Petersburg, Moscow and Tobolsk; she granted new privileges to the Academy; she founded schools in all the towns and the country districts; she dug canals, built granite quays, gave a legal code, instituted an asylum for foundlings, and, finally, introduced into her empire the boon of vaccination, adopted by the Russians solely through her mighty will, and, for the public encouragement, was the first to be inoculated.

Catherine herself was the source of all these blessings, for she never allowed any one else real authority. She dictated her own despatches to her ministers, who, in effect, were but her secretaries. I am much annoyed that the Duchess d'Abrantès, who has recently published a work on Catherine II., has either not read what the Prince de Ligne and the Count de Ségur have written, or has not given credence to those irrefutable witnesses. If she had, she would have more justly appreciated and admired the qualities distinguishing that great Empress, considering her as a ruler, and she would have paid more respect to the memory of a woman in whom our sex ought to take pride for so many reasons.

Catherine II. loved everything that was magnificent in the arts. At the Hermitage she built a set of rooms corresponding to certain rooms in the Vatican, and had copies made of the fifty pictures by Raphael adorning those rooms. She enriched the Academy of Fine Arts with plaster casts of the finest ancient statues and with a large number of paintings by various masters. The Hermitage, which she had founded and erected quite near her palace, was a model of good taste in every respect, and made the clumsy architecture of the imperial palace at St. Petersburg appear to worse advantage than ever by the contrast. It is well known that she wrote French with great facility. In the library at St. Petersburg I saw the original manuscript of the legal code she gave the Russians written entirely in her own hand and in the French language. Her style, I was told, was elegant and very concise, and this reminds me of an instance of her laconic manner of expression which seems to me quite delightful. When General Suvaroff had won the battle of Warsaw, Catherine at once sent him a messenger, and this messenger brought the fortunate victor nothing but an envelope on which she had written with her own hand, "To Marshal Suvaroff."

This woman, whose power was so great, was at home the simplest and least exacting of women. She rose at five in the morning, lit her fire, and then made her coffee herself. It was even said that one day, having lit the fire without being aware that the sweeper had climbed up the chimney, the sweeper began to swear at her, and to shower the coarsest revilements upon her, believing he was speaking to a stove-lighter. The Empress hastened to extinguish the fire, though not without laughing heartily at having been thus treated.

After breakfast the Empress wrote her letters and prepared her despatches, remaining in seclusion until nine o'clock. She then rang for her men servants, who sometimes did not answer her bell. One day, for instance, impatient at waiting, she opened the door of the room they were in, and, finding them settled down at a game of cards, she asked them why they did not come when she rang. Thereupon one of them calmly replied that they wanted to finish their game—and so they did. On another occasion the Countess Bruce, who was allowed in the Empress's apartments at all hours, came in one morning to find her alone at her toilet. "Your Majesty seems to be without assistance," said the Countess. "How can I help it?" answered the Empress. "My maids all went off. I was trying on a dress which fitted so badly that I lost my temper over it, and so they left me to myself. Not one of them stayed, not even Reinette, my head maid, and I am waiting for them to cool off."

In the evening Catherine would gather about her some of the people of her court she liked best. She sent for her grandchildren, and blind man's buff, hunt the slipper and other games were played until ten o'clock, when Her Majesty went to bed. Princess Dolgoruki, who was among the favoured, often told me with what good spirits and jollity the Empress enlivened these gatherings. Count Stachelberg and the Count de Ségur were invited to Catherine's small parties. When she broke with France and dismissed the Count de Ségur, the French Ambassador, she expressed deep regret at losing him. "But," she added, "I am an autocrat. Every one to his trade." Many persons have attributed Catherine's death to the keen sorrow brought her by the failure of the marriage arranged between her granddaughter, the Duchess Alexandrina, and the King of Sweden. That Prince arrived at St. Petersburg, with his uncle, the Duke of Sudermania, in August, 1796. He was only seventeen years old, but his tall figure and his proud and noble bearing made him respected in spite of his youth. Having been very carefully brought up, he showed a most unusual politeness. The Princess whom he had come to marry, and who was fourteen, was lovely as an angel, and he speedily fell deeply in love with her. I remember that when he came to my house to see the portrait I had done of his bride elect, he looked at it with such rapt attention that his hat fell from his hand.

The Empress wished for this marriage more than anything, but she insisted that her granddaughter should have a chapel and clergy of her own religion in the palace at Stockholm, but the young King, all his love for the young Duchess Alexandrina notwithstanding, would not consent to anything that would violate the laws of his country. Knowing that Catherine had sent for the patriarch to pronounce the betrothal after a ball in the evening, the King remained absent from the ball despite M. de Markoff's repeated calls urging him to come. I was then doing the portrait of Count Diedrichstein. We went to my window several times to see if the young King would yield and go to the ball, but he did not. In the end, according to what Princess Dolgoruki told me, when every one was assembled, the Empress half opened the door of her room and said in a very subdued voice, "Ladies, there will be no ball to-night." The King of Sweden and the Duke of Sudermania left St. Petersburg the next morning.

Whether or no it was the grief arising from this occurrence that cut short the days of Catherine, Russia was soon to lose her. The Sunday preceding her death, I went to Her Majesty after church to present her with the portrait that I had made of the Grand Duchess Elisabeth. She congratulated me upon my work and then said: "They insist that you must take my portrait. I am very old, but still, as they all wish it, I will give you the first sitting this day week." The following Thursday she did not ring at nine o'clock as was her wont. The servants waited until ten o'clock, and even a little later. At last the head maid went in. Not seeing the Empress in her room, she went to the clothes-closet, and no sooner did she open the door than Catherine's body fell upon the floor. It was impossible to discover at what hour the apoplectic shock had touched her; however, her pulse was still beating, and hope was not entirely given up. Never in my days did I see such lively alarm spread so generally. For my part I was so seized with pain and terror when apprised of the dreadful tidings that my convalescing daughter, perceiving my state of prostration, became again ill.

After dinner I hastened to Princess Dolgoruki's, whither Count Cobentzel brought us the news every ten minutes from the palace. Our anxiety continued to grow, and was unbearable for everybody, since not only did the nation worship Catherine, but it had an awful dread of being governed by Paul. Toward evening Paul arrived from a place near St. Petersburg, where he lived most of the time. When he saw his mother lying senseless, nature for a moment asserted her rights; he approached the Empress, kissed her hand, and shed some tears. Catherine II. finally expired at nine o'clock on the evening of November 17, 1796. Count Cobentzel who saw her breathe her last sigh, at once came to inform us that she had ceased to live.

I confess that I did not leave Princess Dolgoruki's devoid of fear, in view of the general talk as to a probable revolution against Paul. The immense mob I saw on my way home in the palace square by no means tended to comfort me; nevertheless, all those people were so quiet that I soon concluded, and rightly, we had nothing to fear for the moment. The next morning the populace gathered again at the same place, giving vent to its grief under Catherine's windows in heartrending cries. Old men and young, as well as children, called to their "matusha" (little mother), and between their sobs lamented that they had lost everything. This day was the more depressing as it augured so sadly for the Prince succeeding to the throne.

The Empress's body was exposed six weeks in a large room at the palace, lit up day and night and gorgeously decorated. Catherine was laid out on a bed of state and surrounded by shields bearing the arms of all the towns in the empire. Her face was uncovered, her beautiful hand resting on the bed. All the ladies—of whom some took turn in watching by the body—bent to kiss that hand, or pretended to. I, who had never kissed it in her lifetime, did not dare to kiss it now, and even avoided looking at Catherine's face, which would have left too bad an impression on my memory.

After his mother's death, Paul at once had his father Peter disinterred; he had been buried for thirty-five years in the convent of Alexander Nevski. Nothing was found in the coffin but bones and a sleeve of Peter's uniform. Paul desired the same honours rendered to these remains as to Catherine's. He had them exhibited in the middle of the Church at Kazan; the watch service was performed by old officers, friends of Peter III, whom his son had pressed to come, and whom he loaded

with honours. The day of the funeral having arrived,
Peter III.'s coffin, on which his son had placed a crown,
was put with great ceremony beside Catherine's, and
both were conveyed to the Citadel, Peter's preceding,
it being Paul's wish to humble his mother's ashes. I saw
the marvellous procession from my window as one sees
a play from a box in the theatre. Before the Emperor's
coffin rode a horseman of the guard, clad from top to toe
in golden armour; but the man riding in front of the
Empress's coffin wore only steel armour. The murderers
of Peter III. were, by order of his son, obliged to act as
pall-bearers. The new Emperor walked in the procession
on foot, bareheaded, with his wife and the whole court,
which was very numerous, and attired in deep mourning.
The women wore long trains and enormous black veils.
They were obliged to walk in the snow, at a very low
temperature, from the palace to the fortress, where
Russia's sovereigns were laid to rest, a long distance on
the other side of the Neva. Mourning was ordered
for six months. The women's hair was brushed back,
and their headgear came to a point on the forehead,
which did not improve their looks at all. But this
slight inconvenience was insignificant compared to the
deep anxiety to which the Empress's death gave rise
throughout the whole empire.

CHAPTER X

The Emperor Paul

ACCESSION OF THE EMPEROR PAUL — HIS ARBITRARY
RULE — HIS CIVILITY TO THE AUTHORESS — A MAN
WHO DID NOT KNOW THE EMPEROR'S ADDRESS —
PAUL'S KINDNESS TO FOREIGNERS — HIS FEAR OF
ASSASSINATION — HIS PERSONAL APPEARANCE — THE
EMPRESS MARIA — VAGARIES OF A HALF-MAD EMPEROR
— A NOBLE PRELATE.

THE Emperor Paul, born October 1, 1754, ascended
the throne on the 12th of December, 1796. What I have
related touching Catherine's funeral is sufficient proof
that the new Emperor did not share the national sorrow; it is well known, besides, that he bestowed the
order of St. Andrew upon Nicholas Zuboff, who brought
him the news of his mother's death. Paul was clever,
well-informed and energetic, but his whims bordered
on insanity. In this unhappy Prince generous emotions
were often followed by outbreaks of ferocity; approval
or anger, favour or resentment, were with him altogether a matter of caprice.

One night I was at a court ball; every one except
the Emperor was masked, both men and women wearing
black dominos. One of the doorways between two rooms
became crowded, and a young man in haste to pass
elbowed a woman, who began to scream. Paul at once
turned to one of his adjutants, saying, "Take that gentleman to the fortress, and come back to tell me that he is
safe under lock and key." The adjutant soon came back

to tell the Emperor that he had executed his order;
"but," he went on, "Your Majesty must know that
the young man is very short-sighted. Here is the
proof." And he produced the prisoner's eye-glasses,
which he had brought with him. Paul, after trying the
eye-glasses, was convinced, and said with feeling: "Go
for him quickly and take him to his parents; I shall not
go to bed until you have come back with the information that he is at home again."

The least infraction of Paul's commands was punished
with exile to Siberia, or at least with imprisonment, so
that, unable to foresee how far lunacy and arbitrariness
combined would go, one lived in a state of perpetual fear.
It soon came to one's not daring to invite company
to one's house. If one would see a few friends, one
was very careful to close the shutters, and when a ball
was given it was agreed that the carriages should be
sent home so as to attract less attention. Everybody's
words and actions were watched to such an
extent that I heard it said there was no social
circle without a spy. Allusion to the Emperor was
usually abstained from altogether. I remember how
one day, joining a very small gathering, a lady who
did not know me and who had just ventured upon
this subject, cut her words short when she saw me
coming into the room. Countess Golovin was obliged
to tell her that she might continue. "You may speak
without fear," she said; "it is Mme. Lebrun." All
this seemed extremely burdensome after living under
Catherine, who allowed every one to enjoy entire liberty
without, however, using the word.

It would take a long time to recount to what futilities
Paul practised his tyranny. He ordered, for instance,
that every one should make obeisance to his palace,
even when he was absent. He forebade the wearing
of round hats, which he looked upon as a symbol of

Jacobinism. The police knocked off with their sticks all the round hats they saw, to the great annoyance of people whose ignorance of the regulation exposed them to being thus unhatted. On the other hand, every one was obliged to wear powder. At the time when this regulation was made I was painting young Prince Bariatinski's portrait, and he had acceded to my request that he come without powder. One day he arrived pale as death. "What is the matter with you?" I asked him. "I have just met the Emperor," he replied, all a-tremble, "I barely had time to hide in a doorway, but I am terribly afraid that he recognised me." There was nothing surprising in Prince Bariatinski's fright. All classes were likewise affected, for no inhabitant of St. Petersburg was sure one night that he would sleep in his bed the next.

For my part, I avow that in the reign of Paul I experienced the greatest fear of all my life. I had gone to Pergola to spend the day, and had with me M. de Rivière, my coachman, and Peter, my faithful Russian servant. While M. de Rivière was walking about with his gun to shoot birds or rabbits—to which, by the way, he never did great harm—I remained on the shore of the lake. All of a sudden I noticed the fire that had been lit to cook our dinner communicate itself to the trees and spread with great rapidity. The trees were close together, and Pergola was close to St. Petersburg! I began to scream dreadfully, calling upon M. de Rivière, and, aided by fear, the four of us succeeded in extinguishing the blaze, though not without severely burning our hands. But we thought of the Emperor, of Siberia, and it may well be imagined how this filled us with zeal!

I can only explain the terror that Paul inspired me with from the fact that it was universal, since I must admit that toward myself he was never anything but civil and considerate. When I saw him for the first time at St. Petersburg he was amiable enough to remember that I had been presented to him in Paris on the occasion of his visit there.   I was very young then, and so many years had since gone by that I had forgotten the incident; but princes as a rule are gifted with a memory for faces and names.   Among the various queer ordinances of his reign, one, to which obedience was very troublesome, compelled both men and women to alight from their carriages whenever the Emperor drove by.   Now, I must add that Paul was to be met with very frequently in the streets of St. Petersburg, as he travelled them perpetually, sometimes on horseback with but slim attendance, and sometimes in a sledge without an escort, without any sign by which he might have been recognised. You were nevertheless obliged to obey his command, under pain of incurring his severest displeasure, and it will be agreed that it was cruel to have to jump out into the snow and stand there, however extreme the cold.   One day when I was out driving, my coachman not having observed his approach, I scarcely had time to exclaim: "Stop! it is the Emperor!" But, as my door was opened and I was about to get out, the Emperor himself descended from his sledge and hastened to stop me, saying in the most gracious manner that his order did not concern foreign ladies, especially Mme. Lebrun.

The reason why even Paul's most favourable whims were not reassuring for the future was that no man was ever more changeable in his tastes and affections. At the beginning of his reign, for instance, he loathed Bonaparte.   Later on he conceived such a great tenderness for him that a portrait of the French hero was kept in his sanctuary and he exhibited it to every one. Neither his dislike nor his favour was lasting. Count Strogonoff, I believe, is the only person he always loved and esteemed.   He was not known to have favourites among the gentlemen of the court, but was very fond of a French actor called Frogères, who was not without talent and rather clever. Frogères went into the Emperor's study at all hours unannounced; they were often seen walking together in the gardens arm in arm, chatting on the subject of French literature, for which Paul had a strong fancy, particularly our drama. This actor was often invited to the small court gatherings, and as he was highly gifted in the art of joking, he made the greatest lords the object of jokes, which amused the Emperor very much, but which probably were very slightly amusing to those at whose expense they were made. The Grand Dukes themselves were not safe from Frogères's naughty pleasantries; in fact, after the death of Paul, he did not venture to appear at the palace. The Emperor Alexander, walking alone one day in the streets of Moscow, met him and called to him. "Frogères, why have you not been to see me?" the Emperor asked him with affable air. "Sire," replied Frogères, freed from his fears, "I did not know Your Majesty's address." The Emperor laughed a great deal over this piece of nonsense, and munificently paid the French actor some arrears in salary which the poor man had up till then not dared to claim.

After dealing for a long time with Paul, it was indeed natural that Frogères should dread the resentment of a sovereign, for Paul was so vindictive that the greatest share of his wrongdoings was attributable to his hatred for the Russian nobility, against whom he had had a grievance during Catherine's lifetime. In this hatred he confused the innocent with the guilty, detesting all the great nobles and taking a delight in humbling any of them he did not exile. To foreigners, on the other hand, and especially to the French, he showed remarkable kindness, and I must here affirm that he always received and treated well all travellers and refugees

coming from France. Of these last some were even
generously assisted by him. I will mention as an instance the Count d'Autichamp, who, finding himself
in St. Petersburg without any resources whatever, had
hit upon the idea of making a very pretty elastic shoe.
I bought a pair, which the same evening I showed to
several women of the court at Princess Dolgoruki's. They
were pronounced charming, and this, together with the
sympathy inspired by the refugee, resulted in immediate
orders for a large number of pairs. The little shoe
eventually came under the notice of the Emperor, who,
as soon as he learned the name of the workman, sent
for him and gave him a fine position. Unfortunately, it
was a confidential post, and the Russians were so offended
that Paul could not leave the Count d'Autichamp in
it for long. But he made amends in such a way as to
secure him against poverty. Several facts of this kind,
I confess, made me more indulgent toward the Emperor
than the Russians were, whose peace was incessantly
disturbed through the extravagant caprices of an omnipo-
tent madman. It would be difficult to convey an idea
of the fears, the discontent and the secret murmurings
of his court, that I had formerly seen so placid and
happy. It may be said with truth that as long as
Paul's reign lasted terror was the order of the day.
As one cannot torment one's fellowmen without being
tormented oneself, Paul was far from leading an
enviable life. He had a fixed idea that he would die
by steel or by poison, and this conviction explains much
of his queer conduct. While going about the streets
of St. Petersburg alone at all hours of the day and night,
he took the precaution to have his broth made in his
room, and the rest of his cooking was likewise done in
the secrecy of his apartment. The whole was superin-
tended by his faithful Kutaisoff, a confidential valet
who had been to Paris with him and was in constant

attendance upon him. This Kutaisoff had entertained
an unlimited devotion for the Emperor, and nothing
could ever change it.

Paul was exceedingly ugly. A flat nose, and a very
large mouth furnished with very long teeth, made him
look like a death's head. His eyes were more than
vivacious, though they often had a soft expression. He
was neither stout nor lean, neither tall nor short, and
although his whole person was not wanting in a sort of
elegance, it must be admitted that his face suggested
opportunity for caricature. Indeed, a number were
made, in spite of the danger that such an amusement
threatened. One of them represented him holding a
paper in each hand. On one was written "order," on
the other "counter-order," and on his forehead "disorder." At the mere mention of this caricature I still
feel a little shiver; for it must be understood that there
were lives in jeopardy, in which the artists' and the
purchasers' were included.

But all I have said did not hinder St. Petersburg
from being a pleasant as well as profitable place of
sojourn for a painter. The Emperor Paul loved and
patronised the arts. A great admirer of French literature, he munificently subsidised the actors to whom
he owed the pleasure of seeing our dramatic masterpieces performed.

Doyen, my father's friend and the historical painter
I have already mentioned, was distinguished by Paul
as he had been by Catherine II. Though very old at
the time, Doyen, who had imposed a simple and frugal
manner of living upon himself, had accepted but a portion of the Empress's generous offers. The Emperor
continued in the path of Catherine, and ordered a ceiling
for the new palace of St. Michael, as yet unfurnished.
The room where Doyen was working was close to the
Hermitage. Paul and all the court passed through it

on their way to mass, and the Emperor rarely returned
without stopping to chat for more or less time with
the painter in quite amiable fashion. I am hereby
reminded how, one day, one of the Emperor's gentlemen-
in-waiting stepped up to Doyen and said: "Permit
me, sir, to make a slight observation. You are painting the hours dancing round the chariot of the sun. I
see one there, in the distance, smaller than the rest;
the hours, however, are all exactly alike." "Sir,"
replied Doyen with cool self-possession, "you are perfectly right, but what you point out is only a half-
hour." The first speaker nodded in assent, and went off
greatly pleased with himself. I must not forget to
record that the Emperor, wishing to pay the price of
painting the ceiling before it was finished, sent to Doyen
a bank-note for a large sum—how much I do not now
remember. But the bank-note was enclosed in a wrapper,
upon which Paul had written with his own hand, "Here
is something to buy colours with; as for oil, there is a lot
left in the lamp."

If my father's old friend was pleased with his life at
St. Petersburg, I was none the less pleased with mine.
I worked without relaxing from morning till evening.
Only on Sundays I lost two hours, which I was obliged
to grant people wishing to see my studio, and among these
there were frequently grand dukes and grand duchesses.
Besides the pictures I have already spoken of, and an
endless succession of portraits, I had sent to Paris for
my large portrait of Queen Marie Antoinette, one in which
I had painted her in a blue velvet dress, and the general
interest it provoked yielded me the sweetest delight.
The Prince de Condé, then at St. Petersburg, on coming
to see it, uttered not a word, but burst into tears.

In respect of social amenity St. Petersburg left nothing
to be desired. One might have believed oneself at
Paris, so many French were there at the fashionable

gatherings. It was thus that I saw the Duke Richelieu and the Count de Langeron again. They were really not residents, the first being Governor of Odessa and the other always travelling on military inspections, but it was different with a host of other countrymen of mine. For instance, I made acquaintance with the amiable and dear good Countess Ducrest de Villeneuve. Not only was this young woman very pretty and very well built, but she had a special charm coming from her great goodness of heart. I often saw her at St. Petersburg, as well as at Moscow, by which I am reminded that one day, when I went to dine with her, an instance occurred of a kind not rare in Russia, but which frightened me excessively. M. Ducrest de Villeneuve came for me in a sledge, and it was so cold that my forehead was quite frozen. I exclaimed in terror, "I shall be able to think no more!" M. de Villeneuve hurried me into a shop, where my forehead was rubbed with snow, and this remedy, employed by the Russians in all similar cases, soon banished the cause of my despair.

I did not neglect the natives who treated me so well, for my French friends and my relations with Russian families were constantly increasing. Besides the numerous persons I have already mentioned, I often saw M. Dimidoff, the richest private gentleman in Russia. His father had left him a heritage of richly productive iron and quicksilver mines, and the enormous sales he made to the government kept on enlarging his fortune. His immense wealth was the cause of his obtaining in marriage Mlle. Strogonoff, a member of one of the most aristocratic and oldest families of Russia. Their union was very happy. They left only two sons, one of whom lives in Paris most of the time, and who, like his father, has a great love for pictures.

The Emperor ordered me to make a portrait of his wife. I represented her standing, wearing a court dress, and a diamond crown on her head. I do not like painting diamonds; the brush cannot render their brilliancy. Nevertheless, in taking for a background a large crimson velvet curtain, I succeeded in making the crown shine as much as possible. When I sent for the picture to finish the details at home, the Empress wanted to lend me the court dress and all the jewels belonging to it, but they were so valuable that I declined to accept the trust, which would have given me too much anxiety. I preferred to finish my painting at the palace, whither I had the picture taken back. The Empress Maria was a very handsome woman; her plumpness kept her fresh. She had a tall figure, full of dignity, and magnificent fair hair. I recollect having seen her at a great ball with her beautiful locks falling at each side of her shoulders and a diamond tiara on the top of her head. This tall and handsome woman walked majestically next to Paul, on his arm, and a striking contrast was thus presented. To all her loveliness was added a sweet character. The Empress Maria was truly the woman of the Gospel; her virtues were so universally known that she perhaps affords the only example of a woman never attacked by slander. I confess I was proud to find myself honoured with her favour, and that I set great store by the good-will she showed me on all occasions.

Our sittings took place immediately after the court dinner, so that the Emperor and his two sons, Alexander and Constantine, were habitually present. These august spectators did not annoy me in the least, especially as the Emperor, who alone could have made me feel any diffidence, was exceedingly polite to me. One day, when coffee was being served, as I was already at my easel, he brought me a cup himself, and then waited until I had drunk the coffee to take back the cup and put it away. Another time, it is true, he made me witness a rather comical scene. I was having a screen put behind the Empress in order to obtain a quiet background. In this moment of intermission Paul began cutting up a thousand antics, exactly like a monkey, scratching the screen and pretending to climb up it. Alexander and Constantine seemed pained at their father's grotesque behaviour before a stranger, and I myself felt sorry on their account.

During one of the sittings the Empress sent for her two youngest sons, the Grand Duke Nicholas and the Grand Duke Michael. Never have I seen a finer child than the Grand Duke Nicholas, the present Emperor. I could, I believe, paint him from memory to-day, so much did I admire his enchanting face, which bore all the characteristics of Greek beauty.

I remember, too, a type of beauty of an altogether different kind—an old man. Although in Russia the Emperor is the supreme head of the church, as well as of the government and the army, the religious power is held, under him, by the first "pope," called "the great archimandrite," who is about the same to the Russians that the Holy Father is to us. While living in St. Petersburg I had often heard of the merit and virtues of the divine occupying this post, and one day some of my acquaintances who were going to visit him, proposing to take me with them, I eagerly accepted their invitation. Never in my life had I been in the presence of such an imposing man. His figure was tall and majestic; his handsome face, whose every feature was endowed with perfect regularity, expressed at once a gentleness and a nobility difficult to describe; a long white beard, falling below the chest, added to the venerable appearance of his magnificent head. His dress was simple and dignified. He wore a long white robe, divided in front, from top to bottom, by a broad strip of black material, which made the whiteness of his beard

stand out admirably.   His walk, his gestures, his glance,
—everything about him commanded respect from the
very first.   The great archimandrite was a superior man.
He had a profound mind and great learning, and
spoke several languages; besides, by reason of his virtues
and kindness he was cherished by all who knew him.
His grave vocation never prevented him from being
affable and gracious toward high society.   One of the
Princesses Galitzin, who was very beautiful, seeing
him in a garden one day, ran to throw herself on her
knees before him.   The old man at once picked a rose
and gave it to her, accompanying it with his blessing.
One of my regrets on leaving St. Petersburg was
my not having done the archimandrite's portrait, for I
believe no painter could ever meet with a finer model.

CHAPTER XI

FAMILY AFFAIRS

PONIATOWSKI, LAST KING OF POLAND — HIS AMIABLE
CHARACTER — THE AUTHORESS'S FACULTY OF PRESAGING
DEATH — PONIATOWSKI, THE NEPHEW — MME. LEBRUN
RECEIVED AS A MEMBER OF THE ST. PETERSBURG
ACADEMY — HER DAUGHTER'S UNTOWARD MARRIAGE
— RESULTING IN ESTRANGEMENT BETWEEN MOTHER
AND CHILD.

I WILL now speak of a man I frequently saw for whom I
entertained a lively friendship, and who, after wearing a
crown, was then living in St. Petersburg as a private
gentleman. This was Stanislaus Augustus Poniatowski,
Poland's last king. In my early youth I had heard
this prince, who had not then ascended the throne, talked
of by people in the habit of meeting him at Mme. Geoffrin's, where he often went to dinner. All his companions
of that date praised his amiability and his good looks.
For his good or his harm—it is difficult to decide which—
he made a journey to St. Petersburg. Catherine II.
showed him every distinction, and helped him with all
her might to become King of Poland. Poniatowski was
crowned in September of the year 1764. But this same
Catherine destroyed her own work and overthrew the
monarch she had so heartily helped. The ruin of Poland
once determined, Replin and Stachelberg, the Russian
envoys, became the actual rulers of this unfortunate
kingdom, and so remained until the day it ceased to exist.
Their court became more numerous than that of the

Prince, whom they continually insulted with impunity, and who was king in name only.

Stanislaus Augustus Poniatowski was kind-hearted and very brave, but perhaps he wanted the necessary energy to hold down the spirit of rebellion reigning in his country. He did everything to make himself agreeable to the nobility and the people, and he partly succeeded. But there were so many disorderly interior elements, in addition to the scheme of the three great neighbouring powers for the seizure of Poland, that it would have been a miracle had he triumphed. He ultimately succumbed and retired to Grodno, where he lived on a pension allowed him by Russia, Prussia and Austria, who had divided his kingdom between them.

After the death of Catherine II., the Emperor Paul invited Poniatowski to St. Petersburg, to be present at his coronation. During the whole ceremony, which was very long, the ex-king was allowed to stand, which, in view of his advanced years, pained everybody there. Paul afterward behaved more civilly when he asked him to stay at St. Petersburg, and lodged him in a marble palace to be seen on a fine quay of the Neva.

The King of Poland was now suitably housed. He created an agreeable social circle for himself, largely composed of French, to whom were added some other foreigners he wished to honour. He was so extremely good as to seek me out, to bid me to his private parties, and he called me his "dear friend," as Prince Kaunitz did at Vienna. Nothing touched me more than to hear him repeat that it would have made him glad to have me at Warsaw while he was still king. I was aware, in fact, how at that time, some one having told him I was going to Poland, he had replied that he would treat me with the greatest distinction. But I am sure that every allusion to the past must have been very painful to him.

He was very tall; his handsome face expressed gentleness and kindness; his voice was resounding, and his walk erect without conceit; his conversation had a particular charm, since he loved and knew literature to a high degree. He was so passionately fond of the arts, that at Warsaw, when he was king, he perpetually went to visit the best artists. He was more considerate than can possibly be imagined. I recollect being given a proof that makes me feel rather ashamed when I think of it. Sometimes, when I am painting, I refuse to see any one in the world but my model, which more than once has made me rude to people coming to disturb me at my work. One morning, when I was occupied with finishing a portrait, the King of Poland came to see me. Having heard the noise of horses at my door, I fully suspected it was he who was paying me a call, but I was so absorbed in my task that I lost my temper so far as to cry out, at the moment he opened my door, "I am not at home!" The King, without a word, put on his cloak again and went away. When I had laid down my palette and recalled in cold blood what I had done, I reproached myself so strongly that the same evening I went to the King of Poland for the purpose of proffering my excuses and asking pardon. "What a reception you gave me this morning!" he said as soon as he set eyes on me. He then immediately went on: "I quite understand how a very busy artist becomes impatient if disturbed, and so you may believe that I am not at all angry with you." He obliged me to remain to supper, and there was no further mention of my delinquency.

I rarely missed the little suppers of the King of Poland. Lord Witworth, the English Ambassador to Russia, and the Marquis de Rivière were likewise faithful attendants. We all three preferred these intimate gatherings to the large mobs, because after supper there was always a delightful round of chat, enlivened especially by the King, who knew a host of interesting anecdotes. One

evening, when I had followed the usual invitation, I was
struck by the singular change I observed in our dear
Prince's appearance; his left eye particularly looked so
dull that I was frightened. At leaving, I said on the
staircase to Lord Witworth and to the Marquis de
Rivière, on whose arm I was, "Do you know, I am very
anxious about the King?" "Why so?" they asked.
"He seemed remarkably well; he talked as he always
does." "I have the misfortune to be a good soothsayer,"
I replied. "I read uncommon trouble in his eyes. The
King will soon die." Alas! I had only prophesied too
well, for the next day the King went down with an attack
of apoplexy, and a few days later was buried in the
citadel close to Catherine. I did not learn of his death
without feeling a very real sorrow, which was shared by
all who had known the King of Poland. I am rarely
mistaken in the meaning of the ocular expression. The
last time I saw the Duchess de Mazarin, who was in
perfect health, and in whom nobody observed the
least change, I said to my husband, "In another month
the Duchess will not be alive." And my prophecy
came true.

Stanislaus Poniatowski never married; he had a niece
and two nephews. His oldest nephew, Prince Joseph
Poniatowski, is well known through his military talents
and the great bravery which have earned for him the
name of the "Polish Bayard." When I knew him at
St. Petersburg he might have been twenty-five to twenty-
seven years old. Though his forehead was already devoid
of hair, his face was remarkably handsome. All his
features, admirably regular, were indicative of a noble
soul. He had exhibited such prodigious valour and so
much military science in the late war against the Turks
that the public voice already proclaimed him a great
captain, and I was surprised upon seeing him how any
one could win so high a reputation at that early age.

At St. Petersburg all vied with each other in welcoming and making much of him. At a great supper given him, to which I was bidden, all the women urging him to have his portrait painted by me, he answered with a modesty conspicuous in his character, "I must win several more battles before I can be painted by Mme. Lebrun."

When I again saw Joseph Poniatowski at Paris I at first did not recognise him, so much was he changed. Into the bargain he was wearing a hideous wig that completed his metamorphosis. His renown had, however, reached such a point that there was no need for him to be distressed at having lost his good looks. He was then preparing to go to war in Germany under Napoleon, to whom he, as a Pole, had become a faithful ally. The heroism he displayed in the campaign of 1812 and 1813 is sufficiently known, as well as the tragic occurrence that ended his noble career.

Joseph Poniatowski's brother resembled him in no way; he was lanky, chilly, and dry. I got a close view of him at St. Petersburg, and remember that one morning he came to my house to look at Countess Strogonoff's portrait, and that he concerned himself about nothing but the frame. He nevertheless manifested great pretensions as a picture fancier, permitting his opinions to be guided by an artist who drew very well, but whose chief distinction was to imitate Raphael's sketches, in consequence of which he harboured a sovereign disdain for the French school.

The King of Poland's niece, Mme. Menicheck, showed herself obliging to me on many occasions, and it was a great pleasure to meet her again in Paris. At St. Petersburg she made me do the likeness of her daughter, then quite a child, whom I painted playing with her dog, as well as the portrait of her uncle, the King of Poland, in a Henri IV. costume. The first portrait I did of that charming prince I kept for myself.

One of the pleasantest reminiscences of my travels is that of my reception as a member of the Academy of St. Petersburg. Count Strogonoff, then Director of the Fine Arts, apprised me of the appointed day for my installation. I ordered a uniform of the Academy, in the shape of an Amazonian dress: a little violet bodice, a yellow skirt, and a black hat and feathers. At one o'clock I arrived in a room leading to a long gallery, at the end of which I perceived Count Strogonoff at a table. I was requested to go up to him. For this purpose I was obliged to traverse the long gallery in question, where tiers of benches had been placed which were full of spectators. But as I luckily recognised a number of friends and acquaintances in the crowd, I reached the other end of the gallery without feeling too much confusion. The Count addressed me in a very flattering little speech, and then presented me, on behalf of the Emperor, with a diploma nominating me a member of the Academy. Everybody thereupon burst into such applause that I was moved to tears, and I shall never forget that touching moment. That evening I met several persons who had witnessed the affair. They mentioned my courage in passing through that gallery so full of people. "You must suppose," I answered, "that I had guessed from their faces how kindly they were prepared to greet me." Very soon after I did my own portrait for the Academy of St. Petersburg. I represented myself painting, palette in hand.

In dwelling on these agreeable memories of my life, I am trying to postpone the moment when I must speak of the sorrows, the cruel anxieties which disturbed the peace and happiness I was enjoying at St. Petersburg. But I must now enter upon the sad particulars.

My daughter had attained the age of seventeen. She was charming in every respect. Her large blue eyes, sparkling with spirit, her slightly tip-tilted nose, her pretty mouth, magnificent teeth, a dazzling fresh complexion—all went to make up one of the sweetest faces to be seen. Her figure was not very tall; she was lithe without, however, being lean. A natural dignity reigned in all her person, although she had as much vivacity of manner as of mind. Her memory was prodigious: everything remained that she had learned in her lessons or in the course of her reading. She had a delightful voice, and sang exquisitely in Italian, for at Naples and St. Petersburg I had given her the best singing masters, as well as instructors of English and German. Moreover, she could accompany herself on the piano or the guitar. But what enraptured me above everything else was her happy disposition for painting, so that I cannot say how proud and satisfied I was over the many advantages she commanded. I saw in my daughter the happiness of my life, the future joy of my old age, and it was therefore not surprising that she gained an ascendancy over me. When my friends said, "You love your daughter so madly that it is you who obey her," I would reply, "Do you not see that she is loved by every one?" Indeed, the most prominent residents of St. Petersburg admired and sought her out. I was not invited without her, and the successes she won in society were far more to me than any of my own had ever been.

Since I could but very rarely leave my studio of a morning, I sometimes consented to confide my daughter to the Countess Czernicheff, in order that she might take part in sledging expeditions, which amused her greatly, and the Countess would sometimes also take her to spend the evening at her house. There she met a certain Nigris, Count Czernicheff's secretary. This M. Nigris had a fairly good face and figure; he might have been about thirty. As for his abilities, he drew a little, and wrote a beautiful hand. His soft ways, his melancholy look, and even his yellowish paleness, gave him an interesting

and romantic air, which so far affected my daughter that
she fell in love with him. Immediately the Czernicheff
family put their heads together and began an intrigue
to make him my son-in-law. Being informed what was
happening, my grief was deep, as may well be imagined;
but unhappy as I was at the thought of giving my daughter, my only child, to a man without talents, without
fortune, without a name, I made inquiries about this
M. Nigris. Some spoke well of him, but others reported
badly, so that the days went by without my being able
to fix upon any decision.

In vain did I attempt to make my daughter understand how unlikely in every way this marriage was to
make her happy. Her head was so far turned that she
would take nothing from my affection and experience.
On the other hand, people who had determined to get my
consent employed all possible means to wring it from
me. I was told that M. Nigris would carry off my daughter and that they would marry at some country inn. I
had little faith in this elopement and secret marriage,
because M. Nigris had no fortune, and the family that
befriended him was not blessed with superfluous money.
I was threatened with the Emperor, and I answered,
"Then I will tell him that mothers have truer and older
rights than all the emperors in the world!" It will
scarcely be credited that the persons intriguing against
me were so sure of making me yield under persecution that
they were already throwing out allusions to a marriage
portion. As I was supposed to be very rich, the
ambassador from Naples came to see me and asked a
sum which far exceeded my possessions. I had left
France with eighty louis in my pocket, and a portion of
my savings I had since lost through the Bank of Venice.

I could have endured the malignant and stupid slanders
which the cabal spread, and which were repeated to
me from all sides; it pained me much more to see my

daughter becoming alienated and withdrawing all her confidence from me. Her old governess, Mme. Charrot, who had already made the great mistake of allowing her to read novels without my knowledge, had totally dominated her mind and embittered her against me to such a degree that all a mother's love was impotent to fight against her sinister influence. At last my daughter, who had become thin and changed, fell ill altogether. I was then, of course, obliged to surrender, and wrote to M. Lebrun, so that he might send his approval. M. Lebrun had in recent letters spoken of his wish to marry our daughter to Guérin, whose successes in painting had been bruited loud enough to reach my ears. But this plan, which had such attractions for me, now could not be carried out. I informed M. Lebrun, making him feel that, having but this one dear child, we must sacrifice everything to her desires and her happiness.

The letter gone, I had the satisfaction of seeing my daughter recover; but alas! that satisfaction was the only one she gave me. Owing to the distance, her father's answer was long delayed, and some one convinced her that I had only written to M. Lebrun to prevent him from assenting to what she called her felicity. The suspicion hurt me cruelly; nevertheless, I wrote again several times, and, after letting her read my letters, gave them to her, so that she might post them herself. Even this great condescension on my part was not enough to undeceive her. With the distrust toward me that was incessantly being poured into her, she said to me one day, "I post your letters, but I am sure you write others to the contrary." I was stunned and heartbroken, when at that very moment the postman arrived with a letter from M. Lebrun giving his consent. A mother might then, without being accused of exaction, have expected some excuses or thanks; but in order to have it understood how entirely those wicked people had estranged my daughter's heart, I will confess that the cruel child showed not the least gratitude at what I had done for her in immolating all my wishes, hopes and dislikes.

The wedding was nevertheless enacted a few days later. I gave my daughter a very fine wedding outfit and some jewellery, including a bracelet, mounted with some large diamonds, on which was her father's likeness. Her marriage portion, the product of the portraits I had painted at St. Petersburg, I deposited with the banker Livio.

The day after my daughter's wedding I went to see her. I found her placid and unelated over her bliss. Being at her house again a fortnight later, I made the inquiry, "You are very happy, I trust, now that you are married to him?" M. Nigris, who was talking with some one else, had his back turned to us, and, since he was afflicted with a severe cold, had a heavy great coat on his shoulders. She replied, "I confess that fur coat is disenchanting; how could you expect me to be smitten with such a figure as that?" Thus a fortnight had sufficed for love to evaporate.

As for me, the whole charm of my life seemed to be irretrievably destroyed. I even felt no joy in loving my daughter, though God knows how much I still did love her, in spite of all her wrongdoing. Only mothers will fully understand me. Soon after her marriage she took the smallpox. Although I had never had that frightful disease, no one succeeded in preventing me from hastening to her side. Her face was so swelled up that I was seized with terror. But it was only for her that I feared, and as long as the illness lasted I thought not of myself for a single moment. At last I was glad to see her restored without being marked in the least.

I then resolved to leave for Moscow. I wanted a change from St. Petersburg, where I had been suffering to such a degree that my health was affected. Not that after

the wedding the wretched stories which had been brought
up against me left any impression. On the contrary,
the people who had blackened my character most
repented of their injustice. However, I was unable to
shake off the memory of the past months. I felt miserable, but kept my trouble to myself; I complained of
no one. I observed silence, even with my dearest friends,
on the subject of my daughter and the man she had given
me for a son, going so far as reticence toward my brother,
to whom I had written frequently since being apprised
by him of another misfortune. Indeed, this period of
my life was devoted to tears: we had lost our mother.

Hoping, then, to obtain relief from so much sorrow
through distraction and a change of scene, I hastened
the life-sized portrait I was then doing of the Empress
Maria, as well as several half-length portraits, and left
for Moscow on the 15th of October, 1800.

CHAPTER XII

Moscow

No more dreadful fatigue can be imagined than that
which awaited me in the journey from St. Petersburg to
Moscow. The roads I counted upon as being frozen—as
I had been led to believe—were not yet in that condition.
The roads, in fact, were terrible; the logs, which rendered
them almost impracticable in severe weather, not being
as yet fixed by the frost, rolled incessantly under the
wheels, and produced the same effect as waves of the sea.
My carriage was half-covered with mud, and gave us such
terrible shocks that at every moment I expected to give
up the ghost. For the sake of some relief from this torture, I stopped half-way at the inn of Novgorod, the
only one on the route, where—so I had been informed—
I should be well fed and lodged. Being greatly in want
of rest, and faint with hunger, I asked for a room. Hardly
was I installed when I noticed a pestilential smell that
made me sick. The master of the inn, whom I begged to
change my room, had no other to give me, and I therefore
resigned myself. But soon, seeming to observe that the
intolerable stench came from a glazed door in the room,

I called for a waiter, and questioned him as to the door. "Oh!" he calmly replied, "there has been a dead man behind that door since yesterday. That is probably what you smell." I waited for no further particulars, got up, had my horses harnessed, and started, taking nothing with me but a piece of bread to continue my journey to Moscow.

I had accomplished but half of the journey whose second part was to be more fatiguing than the first. Not that there were any high hills, but the road consisted of perpetual ups and downs—which I called torture. The climax to my annoyance was that I could not amuse myself with a view of the country through which I was travelling, since a thick fog veiled the scene on all sides, and this always depresses me. If one considers, besides these tribulations, the diet I was restricted to after I had eaten my piece of bread, it will readily be conceived that I must have found the road very long.

At length I arrived in the former immense capital of Russia. I seemed to be entering Ispahan, of which place I had seen several drawings, so much does the aspect of Moscow differ from everything else in Europe. Nor will I attempt to describe the effect of those thousands of gilded cupolas surmounted with huge gold crosses, those broad streets, those superb palaces, for the most part situated so far asunder that villages intervened. To obtain a right idea of Moscow, you must see it.

I was driven to the mansion which M. Dimidoff had been kind enough to lend me. This enormous building had in front of it a large courtyard surrounded by very high railings. It was untenanted, and I promised myself perfect peace. After all my fatigue and my forced diet, my first concern, as soon as I had appeased my hunger, was, of course, to sleep. But, bad luck to it! at five o'clock in the morning I was awakened with a start by an infernal din. A large troop of those Russian musicians

who only blow one note each on their horns had established themselves in the room next to mine to practise.
Perhaps the room was very spacious and the only
one suitable for this kind of rehearsal. I was careful
to inquire of the porter if this music was played every
day. Upon his answer that, the palace being uninhabited,
the largest apartment had been devoted to this purpose,
I resolved to make no change in the customs of a house
that was not my own, and to look for another lodging.

In one of my first expeditions I called on the Countess
Strogonoff, the wife of my good old friend. I found her
hoisted on the top of some very high affair which did
nothing but rock to and fro. I could not imagine how
she could endure this perpetual motion, but she wanted
it for her health, as she was unable to walk. But this
did not prevent her being agreeable to me. I spoke
to her of the embarrassment I was in on account of lodgings. She at once told me she had a pretty house that
was not occupied, and begged me to accept it, but because
she would hear nothing of my paying a rent, I positively
declined the offer. Seeing that her efforts were in vain,
she sent for her daughter, who was very pretty, and
asked me to paint this young person's portrait in payment of rent, to which I agreed with pleasure. Thus,
a few days later, I settled in a house where I hoped to find
quiet, since I was to live there alone.

So soon as I was established in my new dwelling, I
visited the town as often as the rigours of the season would
permit. For during the five months I spent at Moscow,
the snow never melted; it deprived me of the pleasure
of seeing the environments, said to be admirable.

Moscow is at least ten miles round. The Moskva cuts
through the town, and is joined by two other small
streams, and it is really an astonishing sight—all those
palaces, those finely sculptured public monuments, those
convents, those churches, all intermingled with pretty

landscapes and villages. This mixture of urban magnificence and rural simplicity produces an extraordinary,
fantastic effect, which must please the traveller who is
in search of something new. The churches are so numerous in this city that a popular saying runs: "Moscow
with its forty times forty churches." Moscow is supposed to contain 420,000 inhabitants, and commerce must
be on a large scale, because in a single quarter, whose
name I have forgotten, there are six thousand shops. In
the quarter called the Kremlin there stands the fortress
of the same name, the old palace of the czars. This
fortress is as ancient as the town, said to have been built
about the middle of the twelfth century, and is situated
on an elevation at the foot of which flows the Moskva,
but there is nothing remarkable in the style excepting its antiquity. Close to this pile, whose walls are
flanked with towers, I was shown a bell of colossal
dimensions half-embedded in the ground, and I was
told it had never been possible to raise it in order to hang
it in the palace chapel.

The cemeteries at Moscow are stupendous, and following
the custom prevailing all over Russia, several times a
year, but especially on the day that in Russia corresponds
to our Death Day, the cemeteries are filled with vast
crowds. Men and women kneel at their family tombs,
and there give vent to loud lamentations, which may be
heard a long way off.

A habit as universal in Moscow as in St. Petersburg
is the taking of steam baths. There are some for women
and some for men, only when the men have taken their
bath, coming out of it as red as scarlet, they go out and
roll in the snow in the most extreme cold. To this habit
the vigour and sound health of the Russians have been
attributed. It is very certain they know nothing of
chest maladies or rheumatism.

A pleasant walk in Moscow is the market, which is

always to be found provisioned with the rarest and most
excellent fruits.   It is in the middle of a garden, and is
traversed by a broad avenue which renders the place
fascinating.   It is quite proper for the greatest ladies to go
there and do their buying in person.   In summer they
repair thither in carriages, and in winter in sledges.

I had observed that in St. Petersburg society formed,
so to speak, a single family, all the members of the nobility
being cousins to one another.   At Moscow, where the
population and the nobility are far more numerous,
society becomes almost the public.   For instance, you will
find six thousand persons in the ballroom where the first
families meet.   Around this room runs a colonnade on a
platform a few feet above the ground, where the persons
who are not dancing can promenade, and adjoining are
various apartments in which people sup or play cards.
I went to one of these balls, and was surprised at the
quantity of pretty women I found assembled.   I can
say the same for a ball to which Marshal Soltikoff invited
me.   The young women were nearly all of remarkable
beauty.   They had imitated the antique costume I had
suggested to the Grand Duchess Elisabeth for Catherine
II.'s ball.   They wore cashmere tunics edged with gold
fringes; gorgeous jewels held their short upturned sleeves
in place; their Greek head-dresses were for the most part
tied with bands adorned with diamonds.   Nothing could
have been more stylish or luxurious than these costumes;
they beautified even this class of lovely women, of whom
no one was prettier than the next.   One I especially observed was a young person soon after married to Prince
Tufakin.   Her face, whose features were regular and
delicate, wore an excessively melancholy expression.
After her marriage I began her portrait, but was only
able to finish the head in Moscow, so that I carried off the
picture to finish it at St. Petersburg, where, however,
I before long heard of the death of that charming young

lady. She was scarcely more than seventeen years old. I painted her as Iris, seated on some clouds, with a billowy scarf about her.

Mme. Soltikoff kept one of the best houses in Moscow. I had paid her a call upon arrival. She and her husband, who was then Governor of the town, showed me great kindness. She asked me to paint the Marshal's portrait, and her daughter's, who had married Count Gregory Orloff, son of Count Vladimir. At this time I was doing a picture of Countess Strogonoff's daughter, so that by the end of ten or twelve days I had begun six portraits, without counting the likeness of the good and genial Mme. Ducrest de Villeneuve, whom I was charmed to meet again in Moscow, and who was so pretty that I insisted on painting her. An accident that might have cost me my life deprived me of the use of my studio and retarded the completion of all these works.

I was enjoying perfect peace in the house loaned me by Countess Strogonoff, but, as it had not been inhabited for seven years, it was horribly cold. I remedied the evil as far as possible by heating all the stoves to the utmost. In spite of this measure, I was obliged to leave the fire lit in my bedroom at night, and was so frozen in bed, with the shutters hermetically closed, to say nothing of a small lamp burning near me to moderate the air, that I tied my pillow all round my head with a ribbon, at the risk of being stifled. One night, when I had succeeded in going to sleep, I was awakened by suffocating smoke. I barely had time to ring for my maid, who declared that she had put out all the fires. I told her to open the passage door. Scarcely had she obeyed when her candle went out, and my room and the whole apartment was filled with thick, sickening smoke. We broke the windows as fast as we could. Not knowing where this dreadful smoke came from, it may well be imagined how anxious I was. I then sent for one of the men who lit the fires,

and he informed me that another man had forgotten to
open the cover capping the pipes, which is on the roof, I
think.   Relieved from the alarm of having set Countess
Strogonoff's house on fire, I went to look at my rooms,
all upset that I was.   Near the room where I gave my
sittings was a large stove with two doors, in front of which
I had put Marshal Soltikoff's picture to dry.   I found
this portrait so thoroughly scorched that I was obliged to
do it over again.   But what gave me most pain in this
night of trouble was my inability to have removed at once
a collection of pictures by various great masters, sent me
by my husband; they, of course, suffered very much.

By five o'clock in the morning the smoke had only
begun to disperse, and as we had broken the windows the
place was no longer tenable.   But what were we to do?
where to go?   I decided to send to good Mme. Ducrest
de Villeneuve.   She rushed over at once, and took
me off to her house, where I remained a fortnight, during which the dear woman showered attentions upon me
which I shall never forget.   When I had concluded to
go home, I first went with M. Ducrest de Villeneuve to
examine the premises.   Although the windows had not
yet been replaced, the whole house was still so redolent
with smoke that it was impossible to think of living in it
then.   I was exceedingly put out at this, when Count
Gregory Orloff, with that courtesy which is the natural
heritage of the Russians, offered to lend me a vacant
house belonging to him.   I accepted his offer, and immediately went to settle in my new lodgings.   Here,
by the way, the rain poured in so hard that Mme.
Soltikoff, coming to see me and wishing to stay a few
minutes in the room where my pictures were exhibited,
asked me for an umbrella.   But in spite of this new
form of discomfort, I remained in the house until my
departure from Moscow.

The Russian nobles display as much luxury at Moscow

as at St. Petersburg. Moscow possesses a multitude of splendid palaces most richly furnished. One of the most sumptuous belonged to Prince Alexander Kurakin, whom I knew in St. Petersburg, where I had twice painted his portrait. On learning that I was in Moscow, he came to see me, and invited me to dinner with my friends, the Countess Ducrest de Villeneuve and her husband. We found an immense palace, ornamented externally with royal magnificence. Every room through which we passed was more handsomely furnished than the one preceding, and in most of them was a picture of the master of the house, either full or half length. Before leading us to table Prince Kurakin showed us his bedchamber, which surpassed all the rest in elegance. The bed, standing on a raised platform laid with superb carpets, was encircled by richly draped columns. Two statues and two vases with flowers stood at the four corners of the platform; chairs of exquisite taste and divans of great price rendered this room a habitation worthy of Venus. To reach the dining-room we traversed broad corridors, both sides of which were lined with liveried serfs holding torches, which made me feel as though I was taking part in some grave and solemn ceremony. During the dinner invisible musicians overhead diverted us with the horn-playing I have already referred to. Prince Kurakin's large fortune allowed him to maintain the establishment of a king. He was an excellent man, politely obliging toward his equals, and not in the least haughty to his inferiors.

I also dined with Prince Galitzin, universally sought after because of his affable and friendly ways. Although he was too old to sit down to table with his guests, forty in number, the luxurious and very abundant dinner nevertheless lasted more than three hours, which tired me inexpressibly, especially as I was placed opposite a tall window through which came a blinding light. To me this banquet seemed unendurable, but by way of compensation I had the pleasure, before eating, of going through a fine gallery containing pictures by great masters, mixed, it is true, with some that were rather mediocre.   Prince Galitzin, whom age and illness kept to his armchair, had charged his nephew with doing me the honours.   This young man, being ignorant of painting, limited himself to explaining the subjects as best he could, and I had difficulty in refraining from laughter when, before a picture representing Psyche, being unable to pronounce the name, he gave me the information, "That is Fiché."

This long meal at Prince Galitzin's reminds me of another, which probably never ended at all.   I had engaged to dine with a big, stout, enormously wealthy banker of Moscow.   We were eighteen at table; never in my life did I see such a collection of ugly and insignificant faces—typical faces of money-makers.   When I had looked at them all once I dared not raise my eyes again, for fear of meeting one of those visages.   There was no conversation; they might have been taken for dummies if they had not eaten like ogres.   Four hours went by in this fashion, and I was bored to the verge of nausea.   At last I made up my mind, and feigning indisposition I left them sitting at the table—where they perhaps still are.

It was an unlucky day, for that evening a rather comical episode occurred, though it did not amuse me in the least.   For some reason or other I was obliged to make a call upon an Englishwoman.   A lady of my acquaintance took me there, and left me for some time, after promising to come back for me.   As ill-luck would have it, this Englishwoman knew not a word of French, and myself not a word of English, and it may readily be conceived how great was our mutual embarrassment.   I still see her before a little table, between two candles lighting up a face as pale as death.   She thought it her

duty, from politeness, to keep talking to me in a language
I could not understand, and I reciprocated by addressing
her in French, which she understood no better. We
remained together more than an hour, which hour
seemed to me a century, and I imagine the poor
Englishwoman must have found it just as long.

At the period when I was in Moscow the wealthiest
resident of the town, and perhaps of all Russia, was Prince
Bezborodko. He could have raised, it is said, an army of
30,000 men on his estate, so many peasants did he own,
these people, as everybody knows, being considered as
part of the soil in Russia. On his different properties
he owned a large number of serfs, whom he treated with
the greatest kindness, and whom he caused to be
instructed in various trades. When I went to see him he
showed me rooms full of furniture, bought in Paris from
the workshops of the famous upholsterer, Daguère. Most
of this furniture had been imitated by his serfs, and it
was impossible to distinguish between copy and original.
It is this fine work which leads me to assert that the
Russian people are gifted with remarkable intelligence;
they understand everything, and seem endowed with the
talent of execution. Thus the Prince de Ligne wrote:
"I see Russians who are told to be sailors, huntsmen,
musicians, engineers, painters, actors, and who become
all these things according to their masters' wish. I
see others sing and dance in the trenches, plunged in
snow and mud, in the midst of musket and cannon
shots. And they are all alert, attentive, obedient,
and respectful."

Prince Bezborodko was a man of high ability. He
was employed in the reign of Catherine II. and of Paul,
first as secretary to the cabinet, and then, in 1780, as
Secretary of State for Foreign Affairs. In his desire to
avoid the countless appeals by which he was besieged,
he made himself as inaccessible as possible. Women

sometimes followed him into his carriage. He would answer their demands with "I shall forget," and if it was a case of a petition with "I shall lose it." His greatest gift was a thorough and exact knowledge of the Russian language. In addition to this he boasted a phenomenal memory and an astonishing facility of putting his thoughts into words. I give a well-known instance in proof thereof. On one occasion the Empress ordered him to draw up a ukase, which, however, a great pressure of business caused him to forget. The first time he saw the Empress again, after conferring with him on several matters of administration, she asked him for the ukase. Bezborodko, not the least bit in the world dismayed, drew a sheet of paper out of his portfolio, and without a moment's hesitation improvised the whole thing from beginning to end. Catherine was so well pleased with this presentment that she took the paper from him to look at it. Her surprise may be imagined at the sight of a sheet that was quite blank! Bezborodko began elaborate excuses, but she stopped him with compliments, and the next day made him Privy Councillor.

Another Russian, whose memory was as marvellous as Prince Bezborodko's, was Count Buturlin, whom I knew quite well at Moscow, where, by the way, we lived so far apart that whenever I supped with Countess Buturlin I was obliged to go two miles. The Count, through his experience and his knowledge, is one of the most remarkable men I have ever known. He speaks all the languages with extraordinary ease, and his information on all sorts of subjects renders his conversation infinitely fascinating. But his superiority over others never prevented him from being very unaffected, nor from treating his friends with good-nature and generosity. He owned a huge library in Moscow, composed of the rarest and most valuable books in different languages. His memory was such that when he was recounting a

historical or any other anecdote he could at once tell in
what room and on what shelf of his library the book was
that he had just cited. I was greatly amazed at this,
yet a thing as fully astonishing was to hear him talk of
all the towns of Europe and their most conspicuous
features as if he had lived in them a long time,
whereas he had never once set foot outside of Russia.
For my part, I know that he spoke to me about Paris
and its buildings, and everything curious to be seen
there, in such complete detail that I exclaimed, "It is
impossible that you have not been in Paris!"

The request made to me for portraits and my agreeable social circle ought to have kept me longer in Moscow,
where I stayed but five months, of which I spent six
weeks in my room. But I was melancholy and ailing;
I felt a need of rest, especially of breathing in a warmer
climate. I therefore resolved upon returning to St.
Petersburg to see my daughter and then quitting Russia.
I was, however, held back for some days by an unusually
severe attack of my general indisposition.

CHAPTER XIII

Good-by to Russia

DEPARTURE FROM MOSCOW — NEWS OF THE DEATH OF
PAUL — PARTICULARS OF HIS ASSASSINATION — ET TU
BRUTE? — PAUL'S PRESENTIMENTS OF PERIL — HIS
SUCCESSOR NOT AN ACCOMPLICE IN THE CRIME —
ALEXANDER I. A POPULAR MONARCH — AN ORDER FROM
AN IMPERIAL CUSTOMER AND MODEL — FAREWELLS
TO FRIENDS — AMONG THEM, CZAR AND CZARINA.

WHEN I was sufficiently restored I announced my departure and made my adieus. Everything was done to induce me to stay. People offered to pay more for my portraits than I had received in St. Petersburg—to allow me all the time I required to finish them without fatiguing myself. I call to mind now, the very day prior to my leaving, while I was engaged in packing up on the ground floor of my house, there suddenly appeared before me, unannounced, a man of colossal stature in a white cloak, at whose sight I was nearly frightened to death. In Moscow one continually saw people banished to Siberia by Paul, and although but two French had been exiled— both authors of infamous libels against Russia—I forthwith judged this stranger to be an emissary of Paul. I breathed freely only when I heard him beseeching me not to leave Moscow, and begging me to do a large likeness of his whole family. Upon my refusal, which I made as polite as possible, the good gentleman asked me fervently at least to give my own portrait to the town. I acknowledge that this last request so touched my heart as to leave me an enduring regret that my affairs and the state of my health prevented me from complying.

Several persons who, I doubt not, were initiated into the revolutionary conspiracy under progress urged me to defer my departure for a few days, promising they would go to St. Petersburg with me. But in my complete ignorance of the plot, I persisted in starting—in which I made a great mistake. For by waiting a little I might have avoided the hardships I underwent on those abominable roads, again rendered well-nigh impracticable by a thaw.

It was on the 12th of March, 1801, when I was half-way between Moscow and St. Petersburg, that I heard the news of Paul's death. I found in front of the posthouse a number of couriers, who were about to spread the news in the different towns of the empire, and, since they took all the horses, I could obtain none for myself. I was obliged to remain in my carriage, which had been put by the roadside on the bank of a river; such a bitter wind was blowing that it froze me. Nevertheless, I was compelled to pass the night there. At last I contrived to hire some horses, and I reached St. Petersburg only at eight or nine on the morning of the following day.

I found that city in a delirium of joy; people were singing and dancing and kissing one another in the streets; acquaintances of mine ran up to my carriage and squeezed my hands, exclaiming "What a blessing!" They told me that the houses had been illuminated the evening before. In short, the death of the unhappy Prince gave rise to general rejoicings.

None of the particulars of the dreadful occurrence were secret from anybody, and I can aver that the accounts given me that day all agreed. Palhen, one of the conspirators, had taken every means to frighten Paul with a plot he alleged to have been hatched by the Empress and her children for the purpose of seizing the throne.

Paul's habitually suspicious mind incited him only too
strongly to credit these false confidences, which enraged
him to the degree of ordering his wife and the Grand Dukes
to be shut up in the fortress. Palhen declined to obey
without the Emperor's signed authority. Paul gave his
signature, and Palhen at once went to Alexander with
the document. "You see," he said, "that your father
is mad, and that you are all lost unless we forestall him
by locking him up first." Alexander, though believing
his life and his family's in jeopardy, did nothing but
consent through silence to this idea, which seemed merely
to propose putting a lunatic out of harm's way. But
Palhen and his accomplices thought it necessary to go
further. Five of the conspirators undertook the assassination, one of them being Plato Zuboff, a former pet
of Catherine, whom Paul had loaded with favours after
recalling him from exile. The five penetrated into Paul's
sleeping apartment after he had gone to bed. The two
guards at the door defended it valiantly, but their resist-
ance was fruitless, and one of them was killed. At the
sight of the infuriated men rushing in upon him, Paul
rose from his couch. As he was very powerful he made
a long fight against his murderers, who finally managed
to strangle him in an armchair. The unhappy man's
last words were, "You, too, Zuboff! I thought you were
my friend!"

It seems that chance had contributed in every way
to the success of the plot. A regiment of soldiers had
been brought to surround the palace, and the Colonel, far
from being in the counsels of the conspirators, fully
believed that an attempt upon the Emperor's life was to
be frustrated. A portion of the regiment went through
the garden to post themselves under Paul's window.
Unfortunately, the marching of the soldiers did not
awaken him; nor did the noise of a flock of crows, which
were in the habit of sleeping on the roof, and which burst

out cawing. Had it been otherwise, the ill-fated ruler would have had time to reach a secret staircase next to his room, by which he could have descended to that of one Mme. Narischkin, in whom he had full confidence. Having got thus far, nothing would have been easier for him than to make off in a little boat always moored on the canal beside the palace. Besides, the distrust he harboured against his wife had caused him to double-lock the door dividing his apartments from the Empress's. When he tried to escape through that door it was too late, the assassins having taken the precaution to withdraw the key. To crown all, Kutaisoff, his faithful valet, the very day the murder was committed received a letter revealing the conspiracy; but this man had for some time been neglecting most of his duties, and did not open his letters punctually. Kutaisoff left the letter disclosing the conspiracy on the table. On opening the missive next day the unhappy man fell into such a desperate state that he nearly died of it. The same was the case with the Colonel who had placed his troops about the palace. This young officer, Talesin by name, learning of the crime that had been perpetrated, felt such grief at his deception that he went home with a raging fever, which nearly put an end to him. I believe, in fact, that he did not long survive the blow, all innocent that he was. But what I am sure of is that Alexander I. went to see him every day during his illness, and interdicted some firing exercises too near the patient's house.

Although the various impediments I have mentioned might have interfered with Paul's killing, it must be concluded that the contrivers of the scheme never doubted its issue. For all St. Petersburg knew that on the night of the event a handsome young man in the plot named S———ky drew out his watch at midnight among a passably large company, saying: "It must all be over by this time." Paul was dead, indeed; his body was forthwith embalmed, and for six weeks he lay on a bed of state, his face uncovered and showing scarcely a trace of decay, owing to the fact that it was plastered with rouge. The Empress Maria, his widow, went to kneel in prayer every day at the bed. She took her two youngest sons, Nicholas and Michael, such small children that Nicholas one day asked her, "Why is papa always asleep?"

The trick employed to make Alexander I. consent to his father's deposal—for he took no other view of the case—was a fact vouched for to me by Count Strogonoff, one of the wisest and most upright men I have ever known, and the best informed of all as to happenings at the Russian court. He doubted the less how easy it had been to induce Paul to sign the order for his wife's and children's imprisonment, as he was aware by what fearful suspicions the mind of that poor Prince was haunted. The very evening before the assassination there was a grand court concert, at which the whole royal family was present. During a moment's private conversation with Count Strogonoff, the Emperor said to him: "No doubt you think me the happiest of men, my friend. At last I am living in this palace of St. Michael, which I have had built and finely fitted out according to my own tastes. I have my family about me here for the first time. My wife is still good looking, my eldest son is handsome, too, and my daughters are charming. There they are, all of them, opposite me; but when I look at them I see my murderers in them all." Count Strogonoff exclaimed, recoiling, horror-struck: "Some one is lying to Your Majesty! This is an infamous slander!" Paul stared at him with haggard eyes, and then, pressing his hand, declared, "What I have just told you is the truth."

I am firmly persuaded that Alexander knew nothing of the attempt to be made upon his father's life. If all the facts I was acquainted with at the time were not enough, I have conviction from proof afforded by that Prince's well-known character. Alexander I. had a noble, magnanimous heart; not only was he always God-fearing, but he was so honest that even in politics was he never known to resort to guile or deceit. Very well, then—on hearing that Paul was no more his despair was so intense that no one who went near him could doubt his innocence of the murder. The wiliest of men could not have summoned up all the tears he shed. In the first hours of his grief he refused to be Emperor, and I know for certain that his wife Elisabeth threw herself on her knees before him, imploring him to take the reins of government. He then went to his mother, the Empress, who called to him as soon as she set eyes upon him from afar: "Go away! Go away! I see you all covered with your father's blood!" Alexander raised his tearful eyes to Heaven and said, in accents coming from the soul, "I take God to witness, mother, that I did not order this awful crime to be done!" These few words bore such a thorough stamp of truth that the Empress consented to listen to him, and when she learned how the conspirators had cheated her son in the carrying out of their enterprise, she fell at his feet with, "Then I bow to my Emperor!" Alexander lifted her up, knelt before her in turn, took her in his arms and bestowed every mark of respect and affection upon her. Nor did he ever give the lie to this affection. So long as he lived never did the Emperor Alexander refuse his mother anything, and his respect toward her was so great that he insisted on maintaining all the honours of court etiquette for her. Thus she always took precedence before the Empress Elisabeth.

Paul's death occasioned none of the upheavals which too often follow upon the departure of a ruler. All those who had participated in his favour continued to keep the emoluments they owed to his patronage. His valet Kutaisoff, that barber whom he made so rich, whom he had decorated with the highest orders in Russia, remained peacefully in the enjoyment of his master's benefactions. If there was no change in the lot of Paul's friends, it was otherwise with his victims. Exiles were called back, and their property was restored to them; justice was done to all who had been sacrificed to caprices without number. In fact, a golden era began for Russia. It was impossible to deny this at witnessing the love, the regard and the enthusiasm of the Russians for their new Emperor. That enthusiasm was so strong that all esteemed it the greatest thing to have seen, to have met Alexander. If he went walking in the Summer Garden of an evening, or if he passed along the streets of St. Petersburg, the crowd would press about him and call down blessings upon him, while he, the most benevolent of princes, would answer all these demonstrations with perfect graciousness. I was unable to go to Moscow for his coronation, but some people who were there told me that nothing was ever more moving or more beautiful. The transports of popular gladness vented themselves all over the city and in the church. When Alexander placed the diamond crown on the Empress Elisabeth's head, radiant with beauty, they formed such a lovely pair as to evoke unbounded acclaim.

In the midst of the universal elation I was myself fortunate enough to meet the Emperor on one of the St. Petersburg quays a few days after my arrival. He was on horseback, and although Paul's regulations had of course been abolished, I had my carriage stopped for the pleasure of seeing Alexander pass. He rode up to me at once, asked me how I liked Moscow, and whether the roads had given me any trouble. I replied that I regretted having been unable to stay long enough in that glorious city to see all its splendours; as for the roads, I acknowledged they were abominable. He agreed with me, saying he hoped to have them mended. Then, after paying me a thousand compliments, he left me.

Next day Count Strogonoff came to me on the Emperor's behalf, with a command to paint him at half length, and also on horseback. No sooner was this news spread than numbers of court people rushed to my house, asking for a copy of either portrait, they cared not which, so long as they had one of Alexander. At any other time of my life this would have been an opportunity to make a fortune, but alas! my physical condition, to say nothing of the mental sufferings still besetting me, prohibited me from taking advantage of it. Feeling unfit to work at a full-length picture, I did a pastel bust-portrait of the Emperor, and one of the Empress; these I intended to enlarge at Dresden or Berlin, in case I should be obliged to leave St. Petersburg. It was not long, in fact, before my ailments became unbearable; the doctor I consulted ordered me to take the waters at Carlsbad.

I cannot describe the regrets I experienced at leaving St. Petersburg, where I had spent such happy years. It was not without an aching heart that I bade my daughter good-by, bitter though it was to see her estranged from me, to see her completely under the thumb of a clique headed by the vile governess whom I would accuse of everything evil. A few days prior to my departure my son-in-law remarked that he did not conceive how I could quit St. Petersburg at the moment most favourable to my fortune. "You will admit," I answered, "that my heart must be very sick. The reason you can easily guess."

Other separations I likewise found most painful. The Princesses Kurakin and Dolgoruki, that excellent Count Strogonoff, who had given me so many proofs of friendship—that was what I regretted far more than the fortune I was renouncing. I remember how the dear Count came to see me as soon as he heard I was going. He was so perturbed that he walked up and down the studio where I was painting, muttering to himself, "No, no;

she won't go away; it is impossible!" My daughter, who was present, thought he was turning mad. To all the kindly proferred demonstrations of attachment I could not answer except by a promise to return to St. Petersburg. And such was then my firm intention.

When I had quite decided to depart I asked for an audience with the Empress, which was immediately granted, and on presenting myself I found the Emperor there, too. I testified my liveliest and sincerest regrets to Their Majesties, telling them my health compelled me to take the waters at Carlsbad, recommended to me for stoppages. To this the Emperor affably replied: "Do not go so far in search of a remedy. I will give you the Empress's horse, and after riding it for some time you will be cured." I thanked the Emperor a hundred times for the offer, but confessed that I did not know how to ride. "Well," he resumed, "I will give you a riding-master to take you out." I cannot say how touched I was by such kindness, and on taking leave of Their Majesties I sought in vain for terms strong enough to express my gratitude.

A few days after this interview I met the Empress walking in the Summer Garden. I was with my daughter and M. de Rivière. Her Majesty stepped up to me, saying: "Do not leave us, I beg of you, Mme. Lebrun. Remain here and take care of your health. I cannot bear to have you go." I assured her it was my desire and my purpose to return to St. Petersburg for the pleasure of seeing her again. God knows I spoke the truth, but I have, none the less, often been assailed with the fear that my refusal to stay in Russia may have appeared as ingratitude to Their Majesties, and that they may not have quite forgiven me.

On crossing the Russian border I burst into tears. I wanted to retrace my journey, and I vowed I would come back to those who had for so long heaped tokens of friendship and devotion upon me, and whose memory is ever in my heart. But one must believe in fate, for I never again saw the country which I still look upon as a second motherland.

CHAPTER XIV

HOMEWARD BOUND

I LEFT St. Petersburg sad, sick and alone in my carriage,
having been unable to keep my Russian maid. I had
nobody but a very old man who wanted to go to Prussia,
and whom I had given a servant's place through pity,
which I had cause to regret, because he got so drunk at
every stage that he had to be carried back to the box.
M. de Rivière, escorting me in his calash, was of no great
assistance to me, especially after crossing the Russian
frontier and entering the sandy district, for his postilions,
from whom he did not know how to exact obedience,
were continually taking side roads, while I followed the
main road.

My first stop I made at Narva, a well-fortified but
ugly, ill-paved little town. The road leading there is
entrancing; it is edged with pretty houses and English
gardens; in the distance is the sea, covered with ships,
which makes this route extremely picturesque. The
women of Narva wear the dress of ancient times. They
are good-looking, for the people of Livonia in general are
splendid. Nearly all the heads of the old men reminded

me of Raphael's heads of Christ, and the young men, their long hair falling on their shoulders, might have been models to that great painter.

The day after my arrival I went to visit a magnificent cataract at some distance from the town. A huge mass of water—you cannot tell where it comes from—forms a torrent so rapid and powerful that in its course it runs up enormous rocks, from which it tumbles noisily down to rush up other rocks. The multitudinous cascades thus shooting after each other in succession, and swallowing each other up, produce a terrifying din. While I was occupied in sketching this beautiful horror some of the inhabitants of Narva who were watching me told me of a dreadful thing they had witnessed. The waters of the cataract, swollen by great rains, had carried away some of the bank, and with it a house that was the home of a family. The cries of distress of the unfortunates were heard, and their frightful plight was seen, but no aid could be given them, since it was impossible to steer a boat in the torrent. The heartrending spectacle was finally followed by one far more shocking, when the house and the unhappy family were engulfed, and disappeared before the eyes of those who were now narrating the catastrophe, and who were still quite affected by it.

Arriving at Riga, I found that this town, like Narva, was neither handsome nor well-paved, but it is known to be a great commercial place and has a fine harbour. Most of the men are habited like Turks or Poles, and all women not of the populace put a gauze veil over their heads when they go out. I scarcely had time to make other observations, as I was hastening to reach Mittau, where I still hoped to find the royal family. But to my annoyance I arrived too late and did not meet them, so that I made but a short stay in this town, where I had only gone for the sake of seeing our Princes.

I had taken the post from St. Petersburg, but at Riga

we met the Grand Duchess of Baden, who was on her way
to the Empress, her daughter, and who left not a horse
on our route. I was obliged to hire horses at livery-
stables, and the coachman, instead of putting me down
for the night at the posthouses, took me to wretched
cabins where there were no beds and nothing to eat, so
that in most cases I spent the night in my carriage. As
for food, the soup I got was made without meat, but
with carrots and bad butter. If I had a fowl killed it was
so lean and so tough that M. de Rivière and I were unable
to cut it. And we barely had time to finish these miserable meals, in so great haste were the liverymen to resume
the journey. We drove through such deep sand that
the horses went at a walk. It was frightfully hot. In
order to get air I was obliged to leave all my windows
open, and both postilions smoked incessantly; the vile
odour of their pipes sickened me so that I preferred to
walk most of the time they smoked, although I was up
to my ankles in sand. Fortunately, no robbers are ever
met with on these roads. True, I noticed wolves on the
neighbouring heights, but apparently they were afraid
of us, for they always fled when we drew near, and so
did the poor stags, which I frequently saw crossing the
road, when alarmed by M. de Rivière's calash.

In my state of health such hardships were bound to
tell upon me. A few days, in fact, were enough to break
me down to such a degree that not to succumb altogether
it needed all my courage and my lively determination
not to interrupt the journey. I became so weak and
ill that I had to drag myself to my carriage, where I
remained motionless, bereft even of the ability to think.
The only sensation I had was a sharp pain in the right
side, caused by rheumatism, and intensified with every
jolt. This pain was so unbearable that one day, when
we were driving on a road under repair and full of stones,
I fainted away in the carriage.

A part of my torture ended at Koenigsberg. There I took the post as far as Berlin, where I arrived about the end of July, 1801, at ten in the evening. But though I needed rest so badly, I was first to undergo the ordeal of the custom-house. I was made to enter a large, dark vault, where I waited a full two hours. The customs officers then said they wanted to hold my carriage, so as to examine it at night, which would have compelled me to walk to the inn in the pouring rain. I argued with these men in French, and they answered me in German. It was enough to drive one to distraction. They would not even allow me to take out a nightcap and a little vial containing an antispasmodic, of which I certainly would stand in great need after such a trial. I was so hoarse from shouting at the barbarians that I could not speak. At last I obtained permission to leave the custom-house in my carriage, and I went to the "City of Paris" inn with a customs officer, a real demon and dead drunk into the bargain. He opened my luggage and turned everything pell-mell, appropriating a piece of embroidered Indian stuff given me by Mme. Du Barry on my departure from Paris. As I did not wish my "Sibyl" or the studies I had made of the Emperor and Empress of Russia to be unrolled, my carriage was put under seal, and at last I was able to get to bed. Early next day I sent for M. Ranspach, my banker, who settled all my difficulties with the custom-house.

Three days sufficed to rest me from the fatigues of my journey, and I was feeling much better when the Queen of Prussia, who was then absent from Berlin, was kind enough to request my presence at Potsdam, where she desired me to do her portrait. I went. But my pen is incapable of rendering the impression which the first sight of that Princess made upon me. The beauty of her heavenly face, that expressed benevolence and goodness, and whose features were so regular and delicate, the loveliness of her figure, neck, and arms, the exquisite freshness of her complexion—all was enchanting beyond anything imaginable. She was in deep mourning, and wore a coronet of black jet, which, far from being to her disadvantage, brought out the dazzling whiteness of her skin. One must have seen the Queen of Prussia in order to understand how bewitched I was when I first beheld her.

She made an appointment for the first sitting. "I cannot," she said, "give it to you before noon, because the King reviews the troops at ten every morning and likes me to attend." She wanted to lodge me in the palace, but, knowing that this must inconvenience one of her ladies, I declined with thanks and took quarters in a neighbouring hotel, where I was very badly off in every way.

My stay at Potsdam was nevertheless a veritable delight to me, for the more I saw of that charming Queen the more was I sensible to the privilege of being in her company. She seemed to wish to see the studies I had made of the Emperor Alexander and the Empress Elizabeth; I promptly brought them to her, as well as my "Sibyl," which I had stretched. I cannot say how graciously she praised this picture. She was so friendly and so kind that the feeling she inspired was altogether one of affection. I look back with pleasure upon all the marks of favour that Her Majesty showered upon me, even in the slightest matters. For instance: I was in the habit of taking coffee of a morning, and in my hotel it was always atrocious. Somehow I told the Queen about this, and the next day she sent me some that was excellent. Another time, when I complimented her on her bracelets, which were in the antique style, she at once removed them from her arms and put them on mine. This gift was more welcome to me than a fortune would have been;

from that day forth those bracelets have travelled with me everywhere. She was also obliging enough to give me a box at the theatre quite near hers. From this place of vantage I enjoyed, above all, looking at Her Majesty, whose lovely face was like that of a sixteen-year-old girl. During one of our sittings the Queen sent for her children. To my great surprise I found that they were ugly. In showing them to me she said, "They are not pretty." I confess I had not the courage to deny it. I contented myself with replying that their faces had a great deal of character.

Besides the two pastels I made of Her Majesty, I did two others of Prince Ferdinand's family. One of the young princesses, Louise, who had married Prince Radziwill, was pretty and very genial. For some time I had a delightful correspondence with her; I count her as one of the people one can never forget. Her husband was a thorough musician. I remember a surprise he caused me arising solely from a difference in national customs. During my sojourn at Berlin I was taken to a grand public concert, and was amazed to the last degree, upon entering the hall, to see Prince Radziwill performing on the harp! Such a thing would be impossible with us. Never could an amateur, especially a prince, play before any one but his own social circle, and certainly not before people who paid. I suppose in Prussia it was quite usual.

In Berlin I made the acquaintance of the Baroness de Krudener, so well known for her cleverness and her rhapsodical notions. Her renown as an author was already established, but she had not yet gained the reputation of a religious prophet that made her so famous in the North. She and her husband treated me with great civility. I can say the same for Mme. de Souza, the Portuguese Ambassadress, whose portrait I painted at the time.

On first arriving at Berlin I called upon the French
Ambassador, General Bournonville, for I was at last
beginning to consider a return to Paris. My friends,
and particularly my brother, urgently suggested I should
do so. They had easily had my name taken off the list
of exiles, so that I was reëstablished as a Frenchwoman,
which, in spite of all, I had ever remained in my heart.
Although General Bournonville was the first republican
ambassador I visited, I had already seen others. Toward
the end of my stay at St. Petersburg General Duroc and
M. de Châteaugiron appeared at Alexander's court as
envoys of Bonaparte, and I remember hearing the
Empress Elisabeth saying to the Emperor, "When are
we to receive the *citizens* ?" M. de Châteaugiron called
upon me. I was as polite as in me lay, but that tri-
coloured cockade affected me unspeakably. A few days
later they both dined at Princess Galitzin's. At table I
found myself next to General Duroc, who was said to
have been one of Napoleon's intimates. He addressed
not a single word to me, and I did likewise with him. The
dinner I speak of gave rise to a rather amusing incident.
The Princess's cook, wholly ignorant of the French Revolution, naturally took these gentlemen for ambassadors
from the King of France. Wishing to honour them,
after much reflection he bethought himself that the lily
was the emblem of France, and accordingly arranged his
truffles and fillets and sweetmeats in that pattern. This
so took the guests aback that the Princess, fearing no
doubt she was suspected of a bad joke, called up the cook,
and asked him what all the lilies meant. Said the worthy
soul with an air of proud satisfaction, "I wanted to show
Your Excellency that I knew the proper thing to do on
great occasions."

A few days before I said farewell to Berlin the Director-
General of the Academy of Painting most courteously
came to me in person with my diploma as a member of

said Academy. The many tokens of good-will heaped
upon me at the Prussian capital and court would assuredly
have kept me longer had my plans not been definitely
fixed. Hence, being resolved to go, I bade good-by to
that dear, kind, lovely young Queen, all unwitting, alas!
how few years after I was to be shocked with the news of
her death.

At starting from Berlin I was threatened with the loss
of everything I owned, and this is how it happened:

My horses were ordered for five o'clock in the morning.
My man servant must have gone to make his adieus to
some friends, for he did not appear, and in Prussia, as
every one knows, horses do not wait. I got up and dressed
in a thoroughly sleepy condition. Meanwhile the porter
of my hotel, not seeing my man, took my jewel-case down-
stairs with my remaining effects. This jewel-case, which
contained all my diamonds and other ornaments, and
my cash—my whole fortune, in fact—I always had under
my feet when travelling. By the greatest luck, as soon
as I got into my carriage, though half asleep, I noticed
that my feet were not supported as usual. The horses
were just off. I cried out to have them stopped, and
then called to the porter for my jewel-case, purposely
making enough noise to wake the mistress of the house.
And I was successful, for, after some evasions by the porter, the case was brought out. It had been found in a
stable at the back of the yard, all covered with hay. The
incident had given my man time to arrive, and I drove
away in high spirits, as may well be imagined, at having
recovered both my servant and my jewel-case. I record
the adventure thinking it may be useful as a lesson to
absent-minded travellers.

From Berlin I went to Dresden, and then on to Brunswick, where I spent a few days with the Rivière family.
Between Brunswick and Weimar my postilion lost the
way, and we were stuck for hours in the heaviest soil.

I remember that as a truce to my impatience—and more particularly to my appetite—I gathered up some of that wretched earth and tried to model a head with it; I really achieved something that looked like a face. Though furnished with letters for the court at Weimar, I did not present them, but after a day's rest proceeded to Gotha. Here I met an old friend I had known in Paris, Baron Grimm, who very civilly attended to all my wants for the journey, which I did not again interrupt until I reached Frankfort. We were obliged to wait at Frankfort six days, during which I was very much bored. To pass the time I mended my old shirts, and the Lord knows what sort of sewing that was! On reaching Paris I engaged a chambermaid, who remarked, when she saw my mending, "Any one can see that Madame has been in a savage country, for this is sewn like the devil." I laughed and informed her that it was my own handiwork. The poor girl, quite embarrassed, was eager to take back what she had said, but I reassured her by acknowledging that I had never been an adept with the needle.

I will not attempt to describe my feelings at setting foot on the soil of France, from which I had been absent twelve years. I was stirred by terror, grief and joy in turn. I mourned the friends who had died on the scaffold; but I was to see those again who still lived. This France, that I was entering once more, had been the scene of horrible crimes. But this France was my country!

CHAPTER XV

OLD FRIENDS AND NEW

PARIS AFTER THE REVOLUTION — RENEWING OLD
ACQUAINTANCES AND FORMING NEW TIES — RIVAL
BEAUTIES: MME. RÉCAMIER AND MME. TALLIEN — MME.
CAMPAN — AN ENGLISHWOMAN'S SLIP OF THE TONGUE
— SOME DISTINGUISHED FOREIGNERS.

On my arrival in Paris at our house in the Rue Gros
Chenet, M. Lebrun, my brother, my sister-in-law, and
her daughter were awaiting me when I alighted from my
carriage; they were all weeping for joy, and I, too, was
deeply moved. I found the staircase lined with flowers,
and my apartment in complete readiness. The hangings and curtains of my bedroom were in green cloth, the
curtains edged with yellow watered silk. M. Lebrun
had had a crown of gilt stars put over the bedstead, the
furniture was all convenient and in good taste, and I felt
altogether comfortably installed. Although M. Lebrun
made me pay dearly enough for all this, I nevertheless
appreciated the pains he had taken to make my place of
abode agreeable.

The house in the Rue Gros Chenet was separated by a
garden from a house facing the Rue de Cléry, which also
belonged to M. Lebrun. In this second house was a great
room where very fine concerts were given. I was taken
there the evening of my arrival, and as soon as I entered
the place everybody turned in my direction, the audience
clapping their hands, the musicians rapping on their
violins with their bows. I was so touched by this flatter-

ing testimony that I gave way to tears.   I call to mind
that Mme. Tallien was at this concert, radiant with beauty.

My first visitor, next day, was Greuze, whom I found
unchanged.   You would even have said that he had never
undressed his hair, for the same locks waved at each side
of his head—just as before my departure.   I was grateful
for his attention, and very glad to see him again.   After
Greuze came my good friend, Mme. de Bonneuil, as pretty
as ever; the dear creature was preserved in a truly wonderful manner.   She told me that her daughter, Mme.
Regnault de Saint-Jean-d'Angély, was to give a ball the
following night, and that I must come unfailingly.   I
answered that I had no ball dress, and then showed her
that famous piece of Indian stuff given me by Mme.
Du Barry, which had gone through such great adventures
since being in my possession.   Mme. de Bonneuil declared
it admirable, and sent it to Mme. Germain, the celebrated
dressmaker, who immediately made me a fashionable
gown, which she brought me that very evening.   So I
went to Mme. Regnault de Saint-Jean-d'Angély's ball,
and I saw the handsomest women of the period, first
among them Mme. Regnault herself, and next Mme.
Visconti, so remarkable for her beauty of both figure and
face.   While amusing myself with looking over all
these lovely ladies, some one sitting in front of me
turned round.   She was so exquisite that I could not
help exclaiming, "Oh, how beautiful you are!"   It was
Mme. Jouberthon, then portionless, who afterward
married Lucien Bonaparte.   I also saw a number of
French generals at this ball.   Macdonald, Marmont and
several others were pointed out to me.   In fact, this
was a new society.

A few days after my return Mme. Bonaparte called
upon me one morning.   She spoke of the balls at which
we had been together before the Revolution; she was
most cordial, and even invited me to dinner at the

First Consul's. However, the date of this dinner was never mentioned.

My friend Robert soon paid me a visit, and so did the Brongniarts, and Ménageot. I was very deeply touched with the joy testified by the friends and acquaintances who crowded to see me every day. But the pleasure of greeting them all was bitterly mingled with sorrow at learning of many deaths I was ignorant of, for not an individual came who had not lost a mother, a husband, or some relation.

And I had another trial to undergo, worse than all the rest. Good manners demanded a visit to my odious stepfather. He still lived at Neuilly, in a small house bought by my father, where I had often been in my early youth. Everything in the place reminded me of my poor mother and my happy days with her. I found her work-basket just as she had left it. In short, the visit was the more sad for me as I was mournfully inclined. Going to Neuilly, I for the first time recrossed the Louis XV. square, where I still seemed to see the blood of a host of noble victims. My brother, who was with me, reproached himself for not having made our carriage take a different route, since I was suffering beyond belief. At this very day I never pass that square without calling up the horrors it has witnessed—I cannot control my imagination.

The first time I went to the play the house looked exceedingly dull to me. Accustomed as I had been, in France and abroad, to see every one powdered, those dark heads and those men in dark clothes made a melancholy picture. You would have thought the audience had assembled to go to a funeral.

In general, Paris had a less lively appearance to me. The streets seemed so narrow that I was tempted to believe double rows of houses had been built. This was no doubt due to my recent impressions of St. Petersburg and Berlin, where the streets, for the most part, are very wide. But what displeased me far more was still to see "liberty, fraternity or death" written on the walls. These words, sanctified by the Terror, aroused the saddest thoughts in me touching the past, and inspired me with some fears for the future.

I was taken to see a great review by the First Consul in the square of the Louvre. I stood at a window in the museum, and recollect that I refused to acknowledge the tiny man I saw to be Bonaparte; the Duke de Crillon, who was beside me, had all the difficulty in the world to convince me. Here, as in the case of Catherine II., I had depicted such a famous man in the shape of a giant. Not long after my arrival Bonaparte's brothers came to view my works; they were very civil toward me, and said the most flattering things. Lucien, especially, inspected my "Sibyl" quite minutely, and proffered me a thousand praises on account of it.

My first visits were to my good old friends, the Marquise de Grollier, Mme. de Verdun and the Countess d'Andlau, whose two daughters I saw at the same time, Mme. de Rosambeau and Mme. d'Orglande, both worthy of their mother in mind and good looks. I likewise went to see Mme. de Ségur. I found her lonely and dejected; her husband had no post, and they were living in straitened circumstances. Later, when I came back from London, Bonaparte made the Count de Ségur Master of Ceremonies, which gave them an easy life. I remember how, about this time, going to see the Countess Ségur toward eight in the evening, and finding her alone, she said to me: "You would scarcely believe I have had twenty people to dinner. They all went after the coffee." I was, indeed, rather surprised, because before the Revolution most of the guests you had to dinner would remain with you until evening, which I thought much more proper than the new method.

At the same time Mme. de Ségur invited me to a large

musical party at which all the notables of the day came together. Here I had occasion to observe another innovation, which seemed to me no better than the first. I was astonished, when I entered the room, to find all the men on one side and all the women on the other—like hostile forces, you would have said. Not a man came over to our side excepting the master of the house, the Count de Ségur, impelled by his old habits of gallantry to pay the ladies a few compliments. Mme. de Canisy was announced, a very handsome woman, with the figure of a painter's model. And then we lost our only knight, for the Count went to lay himself at the feet of this beauty, and did not leave her the whole evening.

I was seated next to Mme. de Bassano, who had been praised highly to me, and whom I had thus been anxious to see. She seemed very much wrapped up in the diamond monogram given me by the Queen of Naples when I bade that Princess farewell. Moreover, considering me probably as an interloper, since I was neither a minister's wife nor a lady of the court, she spoke not a single word to me, which did not, however, prevent me from looking at her repeatedly and judging her extremely pretty.

The first artist I went to see was M. Vien, who had formerly been created first painter to the King, and whom Bonaparte had recently nominated Senator. He was then eighty-two years old. M. Vien may be regarded as heading the restoration of the French school. After this visit I went to M. Gérard's, already famous for his pictures, "Belisarius" and "Psyche." He had just finished a fine portrait of Mme. Bonaparte reclining on a sofa, which was to add yet more to his reputation in this style of painting. Mme. Bonaparte's portrait made me wish to see that which Gérard had done of Mme. Récamier. So I went to that lovely woman's house, delighted with the chance of making her acquaintance.

One woman there was who rivalled Mme. Récamier in respect of beauty. This was Mme. Tallien. Besides her great beauty, she had great goodness of heart; in the Revolution a host of victims condemned to death owed their lives to the influence she exercised upon Tallien. The rescued ones called her "Our Lady of Good Help." She received me most graciously. Later, after marrying the Prince de Chimay, she inhabited a palatial house at the end of the Rue de Babylone, where she and her husband diverted themselves with giving plays. They both acted very well. She invited me to see one of these pieces, and came to several of my evening parties. I had the felicity, too, at this time, of knowing Ducis, whose admirable character equalled his rare talent. The ease and simplicity of all his ways contrasted so well with the splendid imagination with which Heaven had gifted him that I have never known a more lovable man than this excellent Ducis. The sole regret of his friends was that they were unable to induce him to settle in Paris. But he disliked the city, and the author of "Œdipus" and "Othello" demanded shepherds and pastures to make his life agreeably consistent. The solitary mode of existence he rejoiced in caused me a surprise, or rather a fright, which I shall never forget.

After my return from London I went to see him at Versailles, whither, as I was aware, he had retired. It was in the evening; I knocked at his door, and it was opened to me by Mme. Peyre, the architect's widow, candle in hand. I thought she had died long ago, and I uttered a scream. While I tried to collect my wits she related how she had lately been married to Ducis. At last I understood, and composed myself. She led me to her husband, whom I found alone in a little room on the top floor of the house, buried in books and manuscripts. Nothing in this abode seemed to me either pastoral or pleasant, but by the aid of his imagination

Ducis turned this attic, which he called his "lookout," into a place of delight.

I met Mme. Campan again with much pleasure. She was then playing a somewhat important part in what was soon to become the reigning family. One day she asked me to dinner at Saint Germain, where her boarding-school was established. At table I sat near Mme. Murat, Napoleon's sister, but we were so placed that I could see only her profile, particularly as she did not turn her head in my direction. In the evening the young ladies of the school gave us a performance of "Esther," in which Mlle. Augué, who afterward married Marshal Ney, enacted the leading rôle very well. Bonaparte was one of the spectators. He was seated in the first row, and I posted myself in the second, in a corner, but near enough to observe him conveniently. Though I was in a dark spot, Mme. Campan came to tell me, between two acts, that he had guessed who I was.

I was glad to notice a bust of Marie Antoinette in Mme. Campan's room. I felt grateful to her because of this, and she confided to me that Bonaparte approved of it, which I thought very proper on his part. It is true that at this period there seemed no need for him to have any fears relating either to the past or the future. His victories evoked enthusiasm from the French, and even from foreigners. He had many admirers among the English especially, and I recall one day, when I went to dine with the Duchess of Gordon, she showed me Bonaparte's portrait, saying in French, "There is my zero." As she pronounced French very badly, I understood that she meant "hero," and we both laughed heartily over my explanation of "zero."

The large number of strangers I knew in Paris, and the desire to dispel an unconquerable melancholy, prompted me to give some evening parties. Princess Dolgoruki was anxious to meet the Abbé Delille. So I requested his presence at supper with several other people worthy of listening to him. Though this charming poet had gone blind, he had nevertheless kept his cheerfulness of disposition. He recited some of his beautiful lines to us, and we were all enchanted by them. On another occasion I arranged a supper at which all the great personages of the day were present, and among the ambassadors was M. de Metternich. Then I gave a ball, to which Mme. Hamelin, M. de Trénis, and other renowned dancers came. Mme. Hamelin was regarded as the best dancer in Paris society. Certainly she was exquisitely graceful and fleet of foot. I remember how, at this ball, Mme. Dimidoff danced the Russian waltz so entrancingly that we stood on our chairs to watch her.

Having a suitable room in my house on the Rue Gros Chenet, I conceived the idea of putting in a stage and giving plays. The spectators included all persons of distinction.

In all these gatherings I aimed at paying back the Russians and Germans in Paris a few of the favours they had so thoughtfully and amiably rendered me in their own country. Almost every day I saw Princess Dolgoruki, who had been such an angel to me in St. Petersburg. She enjoyed being in Paris very well. One evening I found the Viscount de Ségur at her house. I had often seen him before the Revolution; he was then young and fashionable, and made a thousand conquests through his personal graces. When I saw him again at the Princess's his face was expressionless and wrinkled; he wore a wig with symmetrical curls at each side, leaving his forehead bald. Another twelve years and the wig aged him so that I could barely recognise him excepting by his voice. Princess Dolgoruki came to see me the day of her presentation to Bonaparte. I asked her what she thought of the First Consul's court. "It is not a court," she replied, "but a power." The thing must of course

have appeared to her in that light, being accustomed to
the court of St. Petersburg, which is so large and brilliant,
whereas at the Tuileries she found few women and a
prodigious number of military men of all grades.

Among all the amusements that residence in Paris
afforded me, I was none the less pursued by innumerable
black thoughts, which assailed me even in the midst of
pleasures. To put an end to such a painful state of
mind, I determined to take a journey. More than once,
while I was at Rome, the newspapers had had it that I
was at London, but the fact was I had never seen that
city. Accordingly, I resolved to go there.

CHAPTER XVI

Unmerry England

LONDON — ITS HISTORIC PILES — AND DULL SUNDAYS —
AND TACITURN PEOPLE — PICTURES BY SIR JOSHUA
REYNOLDS — HIS MODESTY — HOW TO DRY PICTURES IN
A DAMP CLIMATE — THE ARTISTIC VIEW OF A CERTAIN
POPULAR BEAUTY — THE PRINCE OF WALES — HIS
ALLEGED ATTENTIONS TO MME. LEBRUN — THE AUTHOR-
ESS LECTURES AN UNFRIENDLY CRITIC — NEWS OF ONE
OF NAPOLEON'S "ATROCIOUS CRIMES."

I STARTED for London on the 15th of April, 1802. I knew not a word of English. True, I was accompanied by an English maid, but the girl had long been serving me badly, and I was obliged to dismiss her very shortly after my arrival in London, because she did nothing but eat bread and butter all day. Luckily I had brought some one besides, a charming person to whom ill-fortune made the home she had found under my roof very precious. This was my faithful Adelaide, who lived with me on the footing of a friend, and whose attentions and counsels have always been most valuable to me.

On disembarking at Dover I was at first somewhat affrighted at the view of a whole population assembled on the shore. But I was reassured when informed that the crowd was simply composed of curious idlers, who were following their usual habits in coming down to see the travellers land.

The sun was going down. I at once hired a three-horse chaise, and made off forthwith, for I was not without

182

apprehensions, seeing I had been told I might very likely encounter highwaymen. I took the precaution of putting my diamonds into my stockings, and was glad I had done so when I perceived two horsemen advancing toward me at a gallop. What capped the climax of my fears was to see them separate, in order—as I imagined—to present themselves at the two windows of my carriage. I confess I was seized with a violent fit of trembling, but that was the worst that happened.

Vast and handsome though London may be, that city affords less food for the artist's interest than Paris or the Italian towns. Not that you do not find a great number of rare works of art in England. But most of them are owned by wealthy private persons, whose country houses and provincial seats they adorn. At the period I mention, London had no picture gallery, that now existing being the result of legacies and gifts to the nation made within a few years. In default of pictures, I went to look at the public edifices. I returned several times to Westminster Abbey, where the tombs of the kings and queens are superb. As they belong to different ages they offer great attractions to artists and fanciers. I admired, among others, the tomb of Mary Stuart, in which the remains of that ill-fated Queen were deposited by her son, James I. I spent much time in that part of the church devoted to the sepulture of the great poets, Milton, Pope, and Chatterton. This last-named is known to have poisoned himself while dying of starvation, and I reflected that the money laid out upon rendering him these posthumous honours might have sufficed, when he was alive, to insure him comfortable days.

St. Paul's Cathedral is also very fine. Its dome is an imitation of that of St. Peter's, at Rome. At the Tower of London I saw a very interesting collection of armour, dating from the various centuries. There

is a row of royal figures on horseback, among them
Elizabeth, mounted on a courser and ready to review
her troops.   The London museum contains a collection
of minerals, birds, weapons and tools from the South
Sea Islands, due to the famous Captain Cook.

The streets of London are wide and clean.   Broad
side pavements make them very convenient for foot-
passengers, and one is the more surprised to witness
scenes upon them that ought to be proscribed by civilisation.   It is not rare to see boxers fighting and
wounding each other to the point of drawing blood.
Far from such a spectacle seeming to shock the
people looking on, they give them glasses of gin to
stimulate their zeal.

Sunday in London is as dismal as the climate.
Not a shop is open; there are no plays, nor balls,
nor concerts.   Universal silence reigns, and as on that
day no one is allowed to work nor even to play
music without incurring the risk of having his
windows broken by the populace, there is no resource
for killing time but the public walks.   These, indeed,
are very well frequented.

The chief amusement of the town is the assembling of
good company, called a "rout."   Two or three hundred
individuals walk up and down the rooms, the women arm-
in-arm, for the men usually keep aside.   In this crowd
one is pushed and jostled without end, so that it becomes
very fatiguing.   But there is nothing to sit on.   At one
of these routs I attended, an Englishman I knew in Italy
caught sight of me.   He came up to me and said, in the
midst of the profound silence that reigns at all these
parties, "Don't you think these gatherings are enjoy-
able?"   "You enjoy yourselves with what would bore
us," I replied.   I really did not see what pleasure was to
be got out of stifling in such a crowd that you could not
even reach your hostess.

Nor are the walks in London any livelier. The women walk together on one side, all dressed in white; they are so taciturn, and so perfectly placid, that they might be taken for perambulating ghosts. The men hold aloof from them, and behave just as solemnly. I have sometimes come upon a couple, and have amused myself, if I happened to follow them awhile, by watching whether they would speak to each other. I never saw any who did.

I went to the principal painters, and was mightily astonished to see that they all had a large room full of portraits with nothing but the heads done. I asked them why they thus exhibited their pictures before finishing them. They all answered that the persons who had posed were satisfied with being seen and mentioned, and that besides, the sketch made, half the price was paid in advance, when the painter was satisfied, too.

At London I saw many pictures by the renowned Reynolds; their colouring is excellent, resembling that of Titian, but they are mostly unfinished, except as to the head. I, however, admired a "Child Samuel" by him, whose completeness and colouring both pleased me. Reynolds was as modest as he was talented. When my portrait of M. de Calonne arrived at the London custom-house, Reynolds, who had been apprised of the fact, went to look at it. When the box was opened he stood absorbed in the picture for a long space and praised it warmly. Thereupon some nincompoop ejaculated, "That must be a fine portrait; Mme. Lebrun was paid eighty thousand francs for it!" "I am sure," replied Reynolds, "I could not do it as well for a hundred thousand."

The London climate was the despair of this artist because of the difficulty it offers to drying pictures, and he had invented, I heard, a way of mixing wax with his colours, which made them dull. In truth, the damp-

ness in London was such that, to dry the pictures I painted
there, I had a fire constantly burning in my studio until
the moment I went to bed. I would set my pictures at a
certain distance from the fireplace, and often would leave
a rout to go and ascertain whether they wanted moving
nearer the grate or farther away. This slavery was
unavoidable and unendurable.

Concerts were very much the fashion in London, and
I preferred them to the routs, though these afforded an
opportunity to the well-received foreigner—and fortunately I was one—of meeting all the best English
society. Invitations are not by letter, as in France.
Only a card is sent, with the inscription, "At home
such and such a day."

The most fashionable woman in London at this time
was the Duchess of Devonshire. I had often heard of
her beauty and her influence in politics, and when I called
upon her she greeted me in the most affable style. She
might then have been about forty-five years old. Her
features were very regular, but I was not struck by her
beauty. Her complexion was too high, and ill-fortune
had ordained that one of her eyes should be blind. As
at this period the hair was worn over the forehead, she
concealed the eye under a bunch of curls, but that was
insufficient to hide such a serious defect. The Duchess
of Devonshire was of fair size, her degree of stoutness
being exactly appropriate to her age, and her uncon-
strained manner became her exceedingly well.

Not long after my arrival in London, the Treaty of
Amiens was abrogated, and all French who had not lived
in England over a year were compelled to leave the
country at once. The Prince of Wales, to whom I was
presented, assured me that I was not to be included in
this edict, that he would oppose my expulsion, and that
he would immediately ask his father, the King, for a
permit allowing me to remain. The permit, stating all

necessary particulars, was granted me. It mentioned that I was at liberty to travel anywhere within the kingdom, that I might sojourn wherever I pleased, and also that I must be protected in the seaport towns I might elect to stop at—a favour which old French residents of England had great difficulty in securing at this juncture. The Prince of Wales went to the limit of politeness by bringing the document to me in person.

The Prince of Wales might then have been about forty, but he looked older, which was to be accounted for by his stoutness. Tall and well-built, he had a handsome face; his features were all regular and distinguished. He wore a wig very artistically disposed, the hair parted on the forehead like the Apollo di Belvedere's, and this suited him to perfection. He was proficient in all the bodily exercises, and spoke French very well and with the greatest fluency. He was elaborately elegant—magnificently so, to the extent of prodigality. At one time he was reputed to have debts to the amount of £300,000—which were finally paid by his father and Parliament. As he was one of the handsomest men in the United Kingdom, he was the idol of the women.

It was but a little while before my departure that I did his portrait. I painted him at almost full length, in uniform. Several English painters became enraged against me on hearing that I had begun this picture and that the Prince allowed me all the time I asked to finish it, for they had long and vainly been waiting for the same concession. I was aware that the Queen-mother said her son was making love to me, and that he often came to lunch at my house. Never did the Prince of Wales enter my door in the forenoon except for his sittings.

As soon as his likeness was done the Prince gave it to Mme. Fitzherbert. She had it put in a rolling frame, like a large bedroom mirror, so as to move it into any of her rooms—something which I thought highly ingenious.

The anger of the English artists toward me did not stop at talk.   A certain M. ——, a portrait painter, published a work in which he vehemently belittled French painting in general and my own in particular.   Sundry parts of the book were translated to me, and they appeared so unjust and absurd that I could not help springing to the defense of the famous painters whose countrywoman I was.   Accordingly, I wrote to this M. —— as follows:

"*Sir:* I understand that in your work on painting you speak of the French school.   As, from what is reported to me concerning your remarks, I gather that you have not the least idea of that school, I think I must give you some information that you may find serviceable.   I presume, in the first place, that you do not attack the great artists who lived in the reign of Louis XIV., such as Lebrun, Lesueur, Simon Vouet, etc., and Rigaud, Mignard, and Largillière, the portrait painters.   As for the artists of the day, you do the French school the greatest injustice in rating it by its achievements of thirty years ago.   Since then it has made enormous strides in a branch totally different from that signalising its decline.   Not, however, that the man who ruined it was not gifted with a very superior talent.   Boucher was a born colourist.   He had discrimination in composing and good taste in the choice of his figures.   But of a sudden he stopped working except for the dainty chambers of women, when his colouring became insipid, his style affected; and, this example once set, all painters tried to follow it.   His defects were carried to the extreme, as always happens; things went from bad to worse, and art seemed irretrievably destroyed.   Then came an able painter, called Vien, whose style was simple and severe.   He was appreciated by true art-lovers, and regenerated our school.   We have since produced David, young Louis Drouais—who died at Rome, aged twenty-five, just as he seemed to give promise of becoming a second Raphael—Gérard, Gros, Girodet, Guérin, and a number of others I might cite.

"It is not surprising that after criticising the works of David, which you evidently do not know at all, you do me the honour of criticising mine, which you know no better. Being ignorant of the English language, I had not been able to read what you wrote about my painting, and when I was told, without being given the particulars, that you had abused me soundly, I answered that, however much you might disparage my pictures, all the worst you could say of them would be less than I think. I do not suppose that any artist imagines he has attained perfection, and, far from any such presumption on my part, I have never yet been quite satisfied with any work of mine. Nevertheless, being now more fully informed, and knowing that your criticism bears principally on a point that appears important to me, I believe my duty is to repudiate it in the interest of art.

"Patience, the only merit you allow me, is unfortunately not one of the virtues of my character. Only, it is true that I am loath to leave my work. I consider it is never complete enough, and, in the fear of leaving it too imperfect, my conscience makes me think about it a long time and touch it up repeatedly.

"It seems that my lace shocks you, although I have painted none for fifteen years. I vastly prefer scarfs, which you, sir, would do well yourself to employ. Scarfs, you may believe me, are a boon to painters, and had you used them you would have acquired good taste in draping, in which you are deficient. As for those stuffs, those eloquent cushions, those velvets, to be seen in my *shop*, it is my opinion that one should pay as much attention as possible to all such accessories. On this point I have Raphael as an authority, who never neglected anything of this kind, who wished everything to be explicit, to be

rendered minutely—that is the language of art—even
to the smallest flowers in the grass.   I can, furthermore,
quote the example of ancient sculpture, in which not the
most trifling accessories are found neglected: the draped
scarfs which lie so snugly upon nude figures, and of which
mere fragments are bought by real fanciers to-day, the
ornamentation on breastplates, the buskins—all that
is carried out with perfect finish.

"And now, sir, allow me to remark that the word *shop*,
which term you apply to my studio, is scarcely worthy
of an artist.   I show my pictures without having money
asked at the door.   I have even, to avoid that practise"
[then in vogue among the painters of London], "set aside
one day each week for persons of good standing and such
persons as these may see fit to present to me.   I may,
therefore, beg you to observe that the word *shop* is
improper, and that severity never excuses a man from
being polite.

"I have the honour to be, etc."

This letter, which I read to some friends, remained no
secret to London society, and the laugh was not on the
side of M. ——, who, all enmity aside, did not know
how to do drapings.

I met a number of compatriots in England whom I
had known for years.   I had the felicity of meeting the
Count d'Artois once more, at a party given by Lady
Percival, who received a number of exiles.   He had
grown stouter, and I really thought him very handsome.
A few days later he honoured me by coming to see my
studio.   I was out, and I only returned just as he was
going away.   But he was good enough to come back
and compliment me upon my portrait of the Prince of
Wales, with which he seemed highly pleased.   The Count
d'Artois did not go out much into society.   Having but
a modest income, he yet saved money, with which he

helped the poorest of the French. His goodness of heart incited him to sacrifice all his pleasures for charitable purposes.

This Prince's son, the Duke de Berri, often came to see me of a morning. He sometimes appeared with small pictures under his arm, which he had bought at a very low price. What proves how good a judge of painting he was is that these pictures were splendid Wouvermans. But it needed a very fine feeling to detect their merit under the grime that covered them. The Duke de Berri also had a passion for music.

I was at the play in London when the murder of the Duke d'Enghien was announced. Hardly had the news spread through the theatre, when all the women in the boxes turned their backs to the stage, and the piece would not have gone on if somebody had not come in to state the report a false one. We then all resumed our seats, and the play continued, but as we went out it was, alas ! all confirmed. We even learned some particulars of this atrocious crime, which will always leave a terrible blood-stain on Napoleon's career.

Next day we attended the funeral mass celebrated for the noble victim. All of the French, our Princes included, and a large number of English ladies were present. The Abbé de Bouvant gave a most touching discourse on the lot of the unhappy Duke d'Enghien. The sermon ended with an invocation to the Almighty to spare our dear Princes from a like fate. Alas ! the prayer was not heard, for we lived to see the Duke de Berri fall by the dagger of a dastardly assassin.

CHAPTER XVII

PERSONS AND PLACES IN BRITAIN

ENGLISH PALACES — AND SCENERY — SUBURBAN PRINCES
—RICHMOND TERRACE—AN ECCENTRIC MARGRAVINE—
THE CHARM OF THE ISLE OF WIGHT — THE BRITONS A
STOLID NATION — THEIR INDIFFERENCE TO RAIN.

ALTHOUGH the kind treatment I received induced me to
stay three years in London, whereas I had intended to
pass but three months, the climate of that town seemed
very melancholy to me. It even disagreed with my
health, and I seized every opportunity to take a breath
of pure air in the lovely vales and dales of England, where
I could at least see some sunlight. I began, shortly after
my arrival, by spending a fortnight with Mme. Chinnery
at Gillwell, where I found the celebrated Viotti. The
house was most luxurious, and I was given a charming
welcome. On reaching the place I saw that the gate was
garlanded with flowery wreaths twined about the pillars.
On the staircase, similarly decorated, stood at intervals
little marble cupids, holding vases filled with roses. In
short, it was a springtime fairy pageant. So soon as I
had entered the drawing-room, two little angels, Mme.
Chinnery's son and daughter, sang a delicious piece of
music to me, composed for me by that good-natured
Viotti. I was truly touched by this affectionate greeting; indeed, the fortnight I spent at Gillwell were days
of joy and gladness. Mme. Chinnery was a beautiful
woman, with much mental subtlety and charm. Her
daughter, then fourteen years of age, played the piano

astonishingly, so that every evening this young girl, Viotti, and Mme. Chinnery, herself an excellent musician, gave us a delightful concert.

I recollect that my hostess's son, though yet a child, had a veritable passion for study. He could not be made to lay his books aside. When his hours of recreation came, and I told him to go out and play with his sister, he would reply, "I am playing." At the age of eighteen the young man had already earned so much credit that at the Restoration he was charged with reviewing all the accounts of the expenditure occasioned by the stay of the English army in France.

I was not tardy in making other excursions to the surroundings of London, and these excursions absorbed all the time I could spare for pleasure.

At Windsor, the royal residence, I admired only the park, which is very fine. The King enjoyed walking on a splendid terrace, whence a magnificent and extensive view is to be got. Hampton Court is another royal castle. Here I saw superb stained-glass windows, which are very old, and which I thought superior to any I had seen hitherto. I also found some grand pictures and some large cartoons, done by Raphael, which I could not admire enough. The cartoons were on the floor, so that I knelt before them such a long time that the custodian was surprised. In the galleries I was shown armour and weapons dating back to remote ages; then, in the gardens, gorgeous yellow rose-bushes, and finally a gigantic vine, enclosed in a hothouse, that in some year or other yielded 1,500 pounds of grapes.

I went with Prince Bariatinski and a few other Russians to pay a visit to the famous Doctor Herschel. This renowned astronomer lived in strict seclusion at some distance from London. His sister, who was always with him, aided him in his astronomical researches, and one was fully worthy of the other, both in learning and noble simplicity. Near the staircase we found a telescope almost large enough to walk about in. The Doctor greeted us with the warmest cordiality. He was obliging enough to let us see the sun through a dark glass, pointing out the two spots discernible upon it, one of which is considerable in size. At night he showed us the planet he had discovered that bears his name. We also inspected at his house a chart of the moon, very detailed, with the mountains, ravines and rivers represented which make that planet resemble the globe we inhabit. In fact, the whole stretch of our visit went by without a dull moment; my Russian companions, Adelaide and myself were all delighted with it.

One cannot speak about the environs of London without calling to mind several fine English watering-places.

Matlock, for instance, offers the precise aspect of a Swiss landscape. On one side of the promenade are highly effective rocks, grown with variegated shrubs, and on the other rich meadows. This English vegetation is truly lovely; it all presents an enchanting view to the eye of those who love nature's beauty. I remember following the bank of a stream so dainty and limpid that I could not tear myself away from it.

Tunbridge Wells, where one also takes the waters, is likewise a very picturesque place. It is true that although one may enjoy the morning rambles in the beautiful neighbourhood, in the evenings one is much wearied by the social gatherings, which are quite numerous. People came together for meals, and after supper, as after dinner, every one would rise and sing "God Save the King," a prayer for His Majesty, which moved me to tears through the sad comparison it prompted me to make between England and France.

Brighton was still better known than either Tunbridge Wells or Matlock. Brighton, where the Prince of Wales had then taken up his residence, is a rather pretty town

opposite Dieppe, with the shores of France visible. At
the time I was there the English feared a descent by the
French. The generals were perpetually reviewing the
militia, who were forever marching about with drums
beating, making an infernal din. I took some delightful walks at Brighton by the seashore. One day I
witnessed a singular phenomenon; the fog was so
thick that the ships off the coast looked as if they were
suspended in the air.

I spent a few days at Knowles Castle, which, after
once belonging to Queen Elizabeth, is now the property
of Lady Dorset. At the gate of this castle I saw two
huge elm trees, reported to be more than 1,000 years old,
which, nevertheless, still bore leaves, especially at the
top. The park, whose boundary touches a forest, is
remarkably picturesque. The castle contains some very
fine pictures; the furniture is still the same as in the day
of Elisabeth. In Lady Dorset's sleeping apartment
the curtains of the bed are all sprinkled with gold and
silver stars, and the dressing-table is of solid silver.
Lady Dorset, an extremely wealthy lady, had married
Sir A. Wilford, whom I had known as English Ambassador
at St. Petersburg. He had no fortune, but was a fine
figure of a man, with noble and distinguished mien. The
first time we all met for dinner Lady Dorset said to me:
"You will be very much bored, as we never talk at table."
I reassured her upon this point. I told her this was also
my own habit, having for years nearly always eaten
alone. She must have been enormously fond of this
custom of hers, for at dessert her son, eleven or twelve
years old, came in, and she hardly spoke to him; she
finally sent him away without giving him the least sign
of affection. I could not help thinking of the reputation
Englishwomen bear: that usually, when their children
are grown up, they care little about them—which has
been taken to mean that they love only their little ones.

At London I renewed acquaintance with the amiable Count de Vaudreuil. I found him greatly changed and fallen off, through all that he had suffered for France. He had married his niece in England, and I went to see her at Twickenham, where she was settled. The Countess de Vaudreuil was young and pretty. She had exquisite blue eyes, a sweet face, and the most striking freshness. Her invitation to pass a few days at Twickenham I accepted, and while there I did a portrait of her two sons.

His Highness the Duke d'Orléans lived near-by; the Count de Vaudreuil, whom the Duke d'Orléans had shown special marks of favour, took me to see him. We found that prince, whose chief delight was his studies, seated at a long table covered with books, one of them lying open before him. During the visit he pointed out to me a landscape painted by his brother, the Duke de Montpensier, whose acquaintance I also made while staying with Mme. de Vaudreuil. As for the youngest of these princes, the Duke de Beaujolais, I only met him out walking; he seemed to have a passably good face and to be very lively. The Duke de Montpensier sometimes came for me, and we would go out sketching together. He took me to the terrace at Richmond, whence the view is magnificent. From that eminence you survey a considerable part of the river's course. We also went over the lovely meadow where the trunk of the tree under which Milton sat may still be seen. It was there, so I was informed, that he composed his poem of " Paradise Lost." Altogether, the surroundings of Twickenham were highly interesting; the Duke de Montpensier knew them to perfection, and I congratulated myself on having him for my guide, the more as this young prince was exceedingly kind and sympathetic.

I had engaged to paint a portrait of the Margravine of Anspach, who asked me to stay with her for a few days in the country so that I might redeem my promise.

As I had heard that the Margravine was an eccentric woman, who would not allow me a moment's peace, would have me waked at five every morning, and do a thousand equally intolerable things, I accepted her invitation only after stipulating certain terms. First I requested a room where I should hear no noises, on the ground that I wished to get up late. Then I warned her that in case we went driving anywhere I never talked in a carriage, and that I preferred walking alone. The good lady agreed to everything and kept her word religiously. If I accidentally came upon her in her park, where she would often be working like a day-labourer, she pretended not to see me, and let me pass without opening her mouth. Perhaps the Margravine of Anspach had been slandered, or perhaps she was obliging enough to put constraint upon herself for my sake; at all events, I felt so much at ease while under her roof that, when I was bidden to another country-place belonging to her, called Blenheim, I went without hesitation. There the park and the house were far better than at Armesmott, and the time went by in a most agreeable manner. Charming evening parties, plays, music—nothing lacked; indeed, though pledged to stay but one week, I remained, instead, three.

I made some expeditions on the water with the Margravine. On one occasion we landed at the Isle of Wight, which stands high on a rock, and reminds one of Switzerland. This island is noted for the mild and gentle ways of its inhabitants. They all live together, I was told, like a single family, enjoying perfect peace and happiness. Possibly now, since a large number of regiments have been in the island, it is no longer the same in respect to the quiet life, but it is a fact that at the time of my visit all the population were well-dressed, civil and benevolent. Besides the suavity I observed in the people, the scenery was so entrancing that I should

have liked to spend my life in that beautiful spot. Only
the Isle of Wight, and Ischia, near Naples, have ever
made me feel such a desire.

I also went to Lord Moira's country seat. Although I
have forgotten the name of his house, I remember how
comfortable everything was and what wonderful cleanli-
ness prevailed all over. Lord Moira's sister, Lady Charlotte, kind and courteous, did the honours with infinite
tact. It was, therefore, unfortunate that the place bored
one. At dinner the women left the table before dessert;
the men remained to drink and talk politics. I can truth-
fully state, however, that at no gathering I attended
did the men get drunk. This convinces me that, if the
custom ever existed in England, it has now ceased as
far as good society is concerned. I may also remark
that I dined several times at Lord Moira's with the Duke
de Berri, and that the Duke never took anything else
than water, far from drinking too much wine, as has since
been alleged.

After dinner we met together in a large hall, where the
women sat apart, occupied with embroidery or tapestry-
work, and not uttering a sound. The men, on their
side, took books to hand, and observed like silence. One
evening I asked Lord Moira's sister, since the moon was
shining brightly, whether we might not walk in the park.
She replied that the shutters were closed and that caution
demanded they should not be reopened, because the
picture-gallery was on the ground floor. As the library
contained collections of prints, my only resource was to
seize upon these collections and go through them, abstain-
ing, in obedience to the general example, from a single
word of speech. In the midst of such a taciturn company,
fancying myself alone one day, I happened to make an
exclamation on coming to a handsome print, which
astonished all the rest to the last degree. It is, nevertheless, a fact that the total absence of conversation

does not preclude the possibility of pleasant chat in England. I know a number of English who are extremely bright; I may even add that I never encountered one who was stupid.

The season was too far advanced when I was at Lord Moira's to allow of my taking long walks. Lady Charlotte proposed to go driving with me, but she went in a sort of cariole as hard as a cart, which I could only endure for a short while. The English are used to braving their weather. I often met them in the pouring rain, riding without umbrellas in open carriages. They are satisfied with wrapping their cloaks about them, but this has its drawbacks for strangers unaccustomed to such a watery state of things. Homeward bound in these English drives, I would sometimes stop on a hill four or five miles from London, hoping for a view of that stupendous city, but the fog lying upon it was always so thick that I never was able to distinguish anything but the tips of its spires.

CHAPTER XVIII

BONAPARTES AND BOURBONS

BACK IN PARIS — THE DEVOTION OF MME. GRASSINI —
CAPRICIOUS, EXACTING MME. MURAT — ASPECTS OF
CHRISTIAN WARFARE — "KILL ALL THOSE PEOPLE!"
LOUIS XVIII. ENTERS THE CAPITAL — THE BARRENNESS
OF NAPOLEON'S VICTORIES — HIS SUCCESSOR'S ATTAIN-
MENTS — BOURBON CHARACTERISTICS — THE AUTHORESS
LOSES HER HUSBAND, DAUGHTER AND BROTHER —
CONCLUSION.

ALTHOUGH I had come to England with the intention
of remaining but five or six months, I had now stayed
nearly three years, held, not solely by my interests as a
painter, but also by the kind treatment bestowed upon
me. I have often heard it said that the English are
lacking in hospitality, but I am far from sharing that
opinion, and harbour grateful memories of the cordiality
I met with in London. Though receiving more social
invitations than I could possibly accept, I nevertheless
succeeded—and this was said to be very difficult—in
forming an intimate circle to my taste. I achieved it
through allying myself with Lady Bentinck and her
sister, the Villiers young ladies, Mme. Anderson, and
Lord Trimlestown, who, an accomplished amateur in the
arts, cultivates painting and literature with taste and
talent, and who, now in Paris, keeps his friendship for
me. I should, therefore, not have decided to return to
France so soon had I not learned that my daughter
had arrived at Paris. I keenly longed to see her again,

the more as I was secretly informed that her father allowed her to form connections that to me seemed improper for a young woman, and hence I hastened my departure. It surely needed a deep motive to resist the appeals which friends and even acquaintances were kind enough to make. As at this period Bonaparte, who had proclaimed himself Emperor, prohibited all English people in France, after the rupture of the Peace of Amiens, from leaving, Lady Herne, well known for her artistic proclivities, said that I ought to be kept back as a hostage.

At the moment I was to get into the post-chaise that was to convey me to the inn near my place of embarkation, the charming Mme. Grassini appeared on the scene. I thought she had simply come to bid me farewell, but she declared she wished to take me to the inn, and made me get into her carriage, which I found full of pillows and packages. "What is all this for?" I inquired. "You are not aware, then," she replied, "that you are going to the worst inn of the world? You may have to wait there a week or more if the wind is not favourable, and I have made up my mind to stay with you." I can hardly say how moved I was at this token of affection. The beautiful woman was leaving the pleasures of London and her friends, to say nothing of the host of admirers always in her train, merely to keep me company. To me this seemed lovable, and I have never forgotten it.

It was a great joy to me to see my friends once more, and especially my daughter. Her husband, whom she had accompanied to France, was charged by Prince Narischkin with the mission of engaging musical artists for St. Petersburg. He left a few months later, but alone —for love, alas! had long since vanished—and my daughter remained, to my great satisfaction. To her misfortune and mine, my child had a very quick temper; besides, I had not been able to instil into her completely

my own distaste for bad company. Add to this that—
whether through my own fault or not—her power over
my mind was great, and I had none over hers, and it
will be understood how she sometimes made me shed
bitter tears. Still, she was my daughter. Her beauty,
her gifts, her cleverness rendered her as fascinating as
possible, and, though I mourned because I could not
persuade her to come to live with me, since she persisted
in seeing certain people I would not receive, I at any rate
saw her every day, and that in itself was a great blessing.

One evening I arranged some living pictures of a kind
which had won warm approval in St. Petersburg, and,
being careful to place behind the gauze none but handsome men and pretty women, the result was charming.
Another day I painted on a screen several head-dresses
of historic characters, making holes under them for the
insertion of a face. The conversation passing with those
who put in their heads amused us vastly. Robert, who
took part in all our gaieties like a schoolboy, put his face
under Ninon's head-dress, which made us laugh like mad.
All these particulars may seem childish to-day, when
evening parties are taken up with talking politics or
playing cards, but some of us had not yet lost the habit
of enjoying ourselves, and the fact is, we enjoyed ourselves
very much. After all, these pleasures were well worth
the cards of Parisian and the stifling routs of London
drawing-rooms.

One of the first people I met, upon my return from
London, was Mme. de Ségur, and I frequently went to
see her. One day her husband told me that my journey
to England had displeased the Emperor, who had curtly
remarked, "Mme. Lebrun went to see her friends." But
Bonaparte's resentment against me could not have been
violent, since, a few days after speaking thus, he sent
M. Denon to me with an order to paint his sister, Mme.
Murat. I thought I could not refuse, although I was

only to be paid 1,800 francs—that is to say, less than half of what I usually asked for portraits of the same size. This sum was the more moderate, too, because, for the sake of satisfying myself as to the composition of the picture, I painted Mme. Murat's pretty little girl beside her, and that without raising the price.

I could not conceivably describe all the annoyances, all the torments I underwent in painting this picture. To begin with, at the first sitting, Mme. Murat brought two lady's maids, who were to do her hair while I was painting her. However, upon my remark that I could not under such circumstances do justice to her features, she vouchsafed to send her servants away. Then she perpetually failed to keep the appointments she made with me, so that, in my desire to finish, I was kept in Paris nearly the whole summer, as a rule waiting for her in vain, which angered me unspeakably. Moreover, the intervals between the sittings were so long that she sometimes changed her mode of doing her hair. In the beginning, for instance, she wore curls hanging over her cheeks, and I painted them accordingly; but some time after, this having gone out of fashion, she came back with her hair dressed in a totally different manner, so that I was forced to scrape off the hair I had painted on the face, and was likewise compelled to blot out a brow-band of pearls and put cameos in its place. The same thing happened with her dress. One I had painted at first was cut rather open, as dresses were then so worn, and furnished with wide embroidering. The fashion having changed, I was obliged to close in the dress and do the embroidering anew. All the annoyances that Mme. Murat subjected me to at last put me so much out of temper that one day, when she was in my studio, I said to M. Denon, loudly enough for her to hear, "I have painted real princesses who never worried me, and never made me wait." The fact is, Mme. Murat was unaware that *punctuality is the politeness of kings*, as Louis XIV. so well said.

Delivered of the vexations arising from Mme. Murat's portrait, I resumed the peaceful life I was accustomed to, but my desire for travel was not yet stilled: I had never seen Switzerland. I therefore resolved to leave Paris once more, and soon was making for the mountains.

In the period succeeding my Swiss travels I at length acquired an inclination for rest. This, together with a taste I had always had for the country, prompted me to leave for Louveciennes before the breaking of the first buds, and consequently I was established there by the time the allies were making their second descent upon Paris. It is well known that the villages fared much worse than the towns at the hands of the foreign troops. I shall never forget the night of March 31, 1814.

Ignorant that danger was so near, I had not as yet considered flight. It was eleven o'clock in the evening, and I had just gone to bed, when Joseph, my Swiss man servant, who spoke German, entered my room, in the belief that I should need protection. The village was being invaded by the Prussians, who were sacking all the houses, and Joseph was followed by three soldiers with villainous faces, who approached my bed with brandished swords. Joseph tried to fool them by saying in German that I was Swiss and an invalid. But paying no attention to him, they began by taking my gold snuff-box, which was on my night-stand. Then they felt under my quilt, to find out whether I had any money concealed, one of them calmly slicing off a piece of the quilt with his sword. Another, who seemed to be French, or at least spoke our language perfectly, said, "Give her back the box"; but far from acceding, his companions went to my desk and seized upon everything it contained. Afterward, the soldiers pillaged my cupboards. At last, after putting me through four hours of mortal fright, these

terrible people quit my house. Nor was this my
only experience of the kind. With the return of the
foreigners in 1815, some English came to Louveciennes.
They robbed me of a number of articles, among them
a magnificent large lacquer box that I sorely regretted
losing, since it had been given me in St. Petersburg by
my old friend, Count Strogonoff.

After the nocturnal visit by the Prussians I wanted
to go to Saint Germain, but the road was not safe
enough, so I took refuge with a good person living at
Marly, near Mme. Du Barry's pavilion. Other women,
frightened like myself, had already chosen this place.
We all dined together and slept six in a room—as far as
sleep was possible. The nights went by with continual
alarms, and I felt the liveliest anxiety for my poor servant,
to whom I owed my life. The faithful fellow had insisted
on staying in my house to hold the soldiers in check.
I had the greatest fears on his account, as the village
was entirely given up to plunder. The peasants camped
in the vineyards and slept on straw in the open air, after
being robbed of all their possessions. Several of them
sought us out, lamenting their misfortunes, and these
mournful tales were recited in Mme. Du Barry's splendid
garden, near the "Temple of Love," amid flowers and
under the brightest of skies! I was so appalled by their
stories and by the incessant cannonading and fusillading
that one evening I attempted to go down into a cellar
and stay there. But I hurt my leg, and was obliged
to come up again.

The last affair happened at Roquencourt. There was
also fighting near Mme. Hocquart's house, very near
the place where I was. We learned that after the combat
the Prussians had sacked from top to bottom the house
of a very Bonapartist lady, who during the fighting
screamed from her terrace to the French, "Kill all those
people!" The victors, having heard her, broke into the

house, and smashed all the mirrors and the furniture as
well, while the lady, in her chemise and without shoes,
was fleeing to Versailles, where she found shelter.

Ultimately, Louis XVIII. entered Paris, ready to
forgive and forget. I went to see him pass on the Quai
des Orfèvres. He was in a carriage, seated beside the
Duchess d'Angoulême. The constitution he had
announced had been greeted with joyful acclamation;
the delight of the people was great and universal. Flags
hung from all the windows on the line of march.
Cries of "Long live the King!" rose to the skies, and
were so loud and heartfelt that I was moved beyond
anything I can say. In the Duchess d'Angoulême's
face was to be read in turn her pleasure at such a welcome
and the painful memories assailing her. Her smile was
sweet but sad—a most natural thing, because she was
following the road her mother had followed in going to
execution, and she knew it. However, the exultation
evoked by the King's appearance and hers went far to
console that afflicted heart. The plaudits pursued them
to the Tuileries, where the crowds filling the gardens
gave vent to the same transports. They sang, they
danced in front of the palace, and when the King showed
himself at the window of the large balcony and kissed
his hands over and over again to the people, their
joy knew no bounds. That evening there was a grand
court reception at the Tuileries; an immense number of
women attended. The King spoke to them all most
graciously and to some cf them even recalled various
incidents creditable to their families.

Possessed of an extreme desire to get a close view of
Louis XVIII., I mingled with the crowd that gathered on
Sunday in the corridor to see him go by on his way to
mass. I was opposite the windows, with the rest, so
that the King could easily distinguish me. When he
did, he stepped over to me, gave me his hand in the most

affable manner, and said a thousand flattering things
about the pleasure he felt in meeting me once more.   As
he remained thus holding my hand for several moments
and addressing none of the other women, the onlookers
must no doubt have taken me for a very great lady,
because, no sooner had the King passed than a young
officer, seeing that I was alone, offered me his arm, and
would not leave me until he had escorted me to my
carriage.

Most of the people who came back with our Princes
were either friends or acquaintances of mine.   It was
very sweet, after all those years of exile, to meet again
in the country of our birth.   But, alas !   This happiness
endured only a few months, for, while we were rejoicing
at our lot, Bonaparte was landing at Cannes.   At midnight, on the 19th of March, 1815, Louis XVIII. and
the whole royal family left Paris.   Napoleon entered
the next day, at eight of the evening, resuming possession
of the Tuileries, the troops filling the courtyards, giving
our Princes' palace the aspect of a castle taken by assault.
Without offense to the memory of a great captain and
the brave generals and soldiers who helped him to win
such fine victories, one may well ask what Bonaparte's
victories have led to, and whether an inch of the ground
remains to us that cost us so much blood.   What proves
how tired the people were of those eternal wars was their
lack of enthusiasm during the Hundred Days.   The King
returned to Paris on the 8th of July, 1815, amid almost
unanimous rejoicings, since, after all our misfortunes,
Louis XVIII. brought back peace.

Henceforth it was seen how this Prince combined
wisdom and ability with his more brilliant mental
qualities.   Times were critical, and Louis XVIII. was
assuredly the ruler to suit the period.   With much
courage and coolness he united elevation of soul and
great subtlety of mind; all his ways were royal.   He gave

readily and liberally; he was fond of patronising art and letters, which he himself cultivated; his features were by no means devoid of beauty, and so noble was their expression that, infirm though he was, the first sight of him called forth involuntary respect. His favourite recreation was talking about literature with clever people. In his youth he had written very pretty verses, and his style was that of an accomplished man of letters. Knowing Latin perfectly, he liked to converse in that language with our most learned Latinists. His memory was prodigious; he could always repeat the most striking passages of a book read rapidly, of a piece seen once. Ducis, who before the Revolution had occupied a post in Monsieur's household, came out from his retreat at Versailles to present his homage to the King. Louis at once recognised him, welcomed him warmly, and recited the best lines of his "Œdipus," scarcely remembered by the aged author.

His Majesty was himself the author of several political writings and an account of a "Journey to Coblentz." There are also attributed to him the text of the opera "The Caravan" and "The Lutenist of Lübeck," a prose play in one act, given at the Théâtre Francais. He had a strong attachment for the Théâtre Francais. He often went to that playhouse, and especially admired the acting of Talma. Whenever that great actor, happening to be on duty for the week, carried a torch before the King to his box, Louis would regularly stop to talk with him a long time. These conversations were in English, spoken by both as well as their own language. It was reported to me that Talma had said, "I prefer Louis XVIII.'s courtesy to Bonaparte's pension."

Courtesy, in fact, is the greatest charm of princes; it doubles the value of the slightest favour. In this regard His Highness the Count d'Artois was in no way behind his brother. By no means forgotten are the innumerable apt sayings, bearing the corner-mark of kindness, with which he won men's hearts. After his accession to the throne—upon the death of Louis XVIII. —I chanced to be at the Louvre the day he was giving medals to the painters and sculptors. Before presenting them he said, in the most sympathetic manner, "They are not encouragements, but rewards." All the artists were touched by the delicate compliment implied in these words.

As for the Duke de Berri, if he had not quite the same courtesy as his father, he was as clever, especially in that timely quickness of wit so useful to princes. I select one example out of a thousand. The first time he reviewed some troops he heard a few cries from the ranks of "Long live the Emperor!" "Quite right, my friends," was his immediate remark; "every one must live." Upon which the same soldiers exclaimed, "Long live the Duke de Berri!"

His goodness of heart went so far that not only did he interest himself in everything that concerned his friends, but behaved toward the domestics of his household as the father of a family might have done. He was worshipped by his servants, and employed his influence to encourage them in good conduct and in making whatever savings they could. One day, as he was about to enter his carriage, a little kitchen scullion came running up to him with, "Your Highness, I have saved fifteen francs this year!" "Well, my boy, that makes thirty," said the Duke, giving him the sum the boy had mentioned. The Duke de Berri kept his revenues in good order; his heaviest expenses were occasioned by his taste for the arts, a predilection shared by his amiable wife. The Duchess de Berri was fond of encouraging young artists; she would buy their pictures and often order more. Her liberality in paying never made her forget the duty of politeness incumbent upon rank.

She showed model civility in all her dealings with men of talent.

Of the Duchess d'Angoulême I would not venture to speak. What could I say that would not fall short of the truth? The merits of this Princess are known to the whole world, and I fear I should but weaken the future verdict of history. It is equally well known that fate united her with a Prince whose high soul worthily appreciated her.

Such was the family brought back to us by the Restoration. It is for politicians to explain how so many virtues and excellencies were insufficient to preserve the throne to them—my grateful heart cannot but regret them.

Under Bonaparte, the large portrait I had made of the Queen and her children had been relegated to a corner of the palace of Versailles. I left Paris one morning to take a glance at it. Arrived at the royal gate, a guard escorted me to the room which contained the picture, and which was forbidden the public. The custodian who admitted us recognised me from having seen me in Rome, and exclaimed, "Oh, how glad I am to welcome Mme. Lebrun here!" He hastened to turn my picture round, which was facing the wall, since Bonaparte, after learning that many came to look at it, had ordered its removal. The order, as is plain, was very badly obeyed, since the exhibition of the picture continued, and this to such a degree that the custodian, when I wanted to give him a trifle, persisted in declining it, saying that I had earned him enough money. When the Restoration came, this picture was reëxhibited at the Salon. I was keeping for myself another picture representing the Queen, done during the reign of Bonaparte. I had painted Marie Antoinette ascending to heaven; to her left, on some clouds, are Louis XVI. and two angels, symbolising the two children he had lost.

As soon as the peace of my country seemed assured, I abandoned all thoughts of leaving it again, and divided my time between Paris and the country. My liking for my pretty house at Louveciennes was undiminished. I spent eight months of the year there, and in those surroundings my life flowed as smoothly as possible. I painted, I busied myself about my garden, I took long, solitary walks, and on Sundays I received my friends. So fond was I of Louveciennes that, wishing to bequeath the place something to remember me by, I painted a picture of Saint Genoveva for the church. Mme. de Genlis was good enough to dedicate a poem to me in acknowledgment. If I gave away pictures, some were given me, and that in the heartiest manner. I had frequently expressed a desire that my friends should commemorate themselves on the panels of my drawing-room at Louveciennes. One fine summer's morning, at four o'clock, while I was asleep, the Prince de Crespy, the Baron de Feisthamel, M. de Rivière, and my niece, Eugenia Lebrun, set silently to work. By ten o'clock each frame was filled. My surprise may be imagined when, upon coming down to breakfast, I entered the room and found it adorned with these delightful paintings as well as with garlands of flowers. It was my birthday. Tears came into my eyes—the only thanks I was able to offer.

In 1819 His Highness the Duke de Berri signified his wish to buy my "Sibyl," which he had seen in my studio at London, and although I perhaps prized this most of all my works, I speedily complied with his request. Some years later I painted Her Highness the Duchess de Berri, who gave me sittings at the Tuileries with the politest punctuality, and besides showed me a friendliness than which none could have been greater. I shall never forget how, while I was painting her one day, she said, "Wait a moment." Then, getting up, she went to her library for a book containing an article in my praise, which she was obliging enough to read aloud from beginning to end. During one of these sittings the Duke de Bordeaux brought his mother a copybook in which his master had written "Very good." The Duchess gave the boy two louis. The little Prince, who might have been about six, began to jump for joy, shouting, "This will do for my poor—and for my old woman first of all!" When he was gone the Duchess told me that her son referred to a poor soul he often met when he went out and of whom he was particularly fond.

While the Duchess sat for me I would become irritated at the number of people who came to make calls. She took note of this and was so considerate as to say, "Why did you not ask me to pose at your house?" Which she did for the two final sittings. I confess that I never could think of such affecting warmth of heart without comparing the time I devoted to this genial Princess with the melancholy hours Mme. Murat had made me spend. I painted two portraits of the Duchess de Berri. In the first she is wearing a red velvet dress, and in the other one of blue velvet. I have no idea what has become of these pictures.

I must now speak of the sad years of my life during which, in a brief space, I saw the beings dearest to me depart this world. First, I lost M. Lebrun. True that for a long time I had entertained no relations whatever with him, yet I was none the less mournfully affected by his death. You cannot without regret be separated forever from one to whom so close a tie as marriage has bound you. This blow, however, was far less than the cruel grief I experienced at the death of my daughter. I hastened to her as soon as I heard of her illness, but the disease progressed rapidly, and I cannot tell what I felt when all hope of saving her was gone. When, going to see her the last day, my eyes fell upon that dreadfully

sunken face, I fainted away. My old friend Mme.
de Noisville rescued me from that bed of sorrow; she
supported me, for my legs would not carry me, and
took me home. The next day I was childless! Mme.
de Verdun came with the news, and vainly tried to
soften my despair. All the wrong-doing of the poor little
one vanished—I saw her again, I still see her, in the
days of her childhood. Alas! she was so young!
Why did she not survive me?

It was in 1819 that I was bereft of my daughter, and
in 1820 I lost my brother. So many successive shocks
plunged me into such deep dejection that my friends,
grieving for my state, urged me to try the distraction
of a journey. I therefore decided to visit Bordeaux.
I did not know that town, and hence the anticipation
changed the current of my thoughts. Nor was I disappointed. My health benefited by the journey, and
I returned to Paris less dark in spirit.

From that day to this I have travelled no more. After
my return from Bordeaux I resumed my daily habits
and my work, which of all distractions I have always
found the best. Although having had the misfortune
to lose so many dear ones, I did not remain forsaken.
I have mentioned Mme. de Rivière, my niece, who,
through her affection and her ministrations, is the blessing
of my life. I must also speak of my other niece, Eugenia
Lebrun, now Mme. Tripier Le Franc. Her studies at
first prevented me from seeing her as often as I should
have liked to, for since her earliest youth her disposition, her mental qualities, and her great gift for
painting had promised to be a joy to me. I took pleasure
in guiding her, in lavishing my counsels upon her, and
in watching her progress. I am well rewarded to-day,
when she has realised all my hopes by her lovely character and her very remarkable talent for painting. She
has followed the same course as myself in the adoption

of portrait painting, and is earning success merited by fine colouring, by great sincerity, and, particularly, by perfect resemblance. Still young, she can but add to a reputation which in her diffidence and modesty she has scarcely ventured to foresee. Mme. Tripier Le Franc and Mme. de Rivière have become my daughters. They bring back all of a mother's feelings to me, and their tender devotion spreads a beautiful charm over my existence. It is among these two dear creatures and the friends who have been spared me that I hope to end peacefully a wandering and even a laborious but honest life.

THE END

APPENDIX

List of Mme. Vigée Lebrun's Paintings

[This list is as complete and accurate as the material available for its compilation allowed. The authoress's own catalogue of her works, which necessarily formed the principal source of information, is itself conspicuous for errors and omissions. To rectify all of these beyond doubt and make an absolutely perfect list would have been impossible.]

FROM 1768 TO 1772

1 Mme. Lebrun's mother, large pastel.
1 The same, back view.
2 Mme. Lebrun's brother as a schoolboy.
1 M. Le Sèvre.
3 M., Mme. and Mlle. Bandelaire.
1 M. Bandelaire, half-length pastel.
1 M. Vandergust.
1 Mlle. Pigale, milliner to the Queen.
1 Her clerk.
1 Mme. Lebrun's mother in white cloak.
1 Mme. Raffeneau.
1 Baroness d'Esthal.
2 Her two children.
1 Mme. d'Aguesseau with her dog.
1 Mme. Suzanne.
1 Countess de la Vieuville.
1 M. Mousat.
1 Mlle. Mousat.
1 Mlle. Lespare.
2 Mme. de Fossy and her son.
2 Viscount and Viscountess de la Blache.
1 Mlle. Dorion.
1 M. Tranchart.
1 Marquis de Choiseul.
1 Count de Zanicourt.
Studies of heads and copies from Raphael, Van Dyck, Rembrandt, etc.

1773

1 M. and Mme. de Roissy.
1 M. de la Fontaine.
1 Count Du Barry.
5 Count de Geoffré.

1 Marshal de Stainville.
3 Mme. de Bonneuil.
1 Mme. de Saint-Pays.
1 Mme. Paris.
1 M. Perrin.
2 Copy of Marquis de Vérac
1 An American lady.
1 Mme. Thilorié, half-length.
1 Copy of the same.
1 Mme. Tétare.
1 Copy of the Bishop of Beauvais.
1 M. de Vismes.
1 M. Pernon.
1 Mlle. Dupetitoire.
1 Mlle. Baillot.

1774

1 Abbé Giroux.
1 Little Roissy.
1 Copy of Chancellor d'Aguesseau.
1 Copy of M. de la Marche.
1 Mme. Damerval.
1 Count de Brie.
1 Mme. Maingat.
1 Baroness de Lande.
1 Mme. Le Normand.
1 Mme. de la Grange.
1 M. Méraut.
1 Viscount de Boisjelin.
1 M. de Saint-Malo.
1 M. Desmarets.
1 Countess d'Harcourt.
2 Mlle. de Saint-Brie and Mlle. de Sence.
1 Countess de Gontault.
1 Mlle. Robin.
1 M. de Borelly.
1 M. de Momanville.
2 The Rossignol sisters.
1 Mme. de Belgarde.

1775

1 Mme. de Monville with her child.
1 Mme. Denis.
1 Count Schouvaloff.
1 Count de Langeas.
1 Mme. Mongé.
1 Mme. Tabari.
1 Mme. de Fougerait.
1 Mme. de Jumilhac.
1 Marquise de Roncherol.
1 Prince de Rochefort.
1 Mlle. de Rochefort.
1 M. de Livoy.

1 Mme. de Ronsy.
1 M. de Monville.
1 Mlle. de Cossé.
1 Mme. Augeard.
1 Copy of Mme. Damerval.
1 Mme. Deplan.
1 M. Caze.
1 M. Goban.
1 Mlle. de Rubec.
1 M. de Roncherol.
1 Prince de Rohan, the elder.
1 Prince Julius de Rohan.
1 M. Ducluzel.
2 Count and Countess de Cologand.
1 Mlle. Julie, who married Talma.
1 Mme. Courville.
1 Marquise de Gérac.
1 Mme. de Laborde.
1 Mlle. de Givris.
1 Mlle. de Ganiselot.
1 M. de Veselay.

1776

1 Princess de Craon.
1 Marquis de Chouart.
1 Prince de Montbarrey.
1 Baron Gros, painter, as a child.
1 Princess de Talleyrand.
1 Count des Deux-Ponts.
1 Mme. de Montbarrey.
1 A banker.
2 M. and Mme. Toullier.
1 Princess d'Arenberg.
1 M. de Saint-Denis.
12 Monsieur, the King's brother.
2 M. and Mme. de Valesque.
1 Little Vaubal.
1 Mme. de Lamoignon.
4 M. de Savalette.
1 Prince of Nassau.
1 Mme. de Brente.
1 Lady Berkely.
1 Mme. Saulot.
1 Countess Potocka.
2 Mme. de Verdun.
1 Mme. de Montmorin.
1 Her daughter.

1777

1 Marquis de Crèvecœur.
1 Baron de Vombal.
1 Mme. Perrin.
1 M. Oglovi.

1 M. Saint-Hubert.
1 Mme. de Nolstein.
1 Mme. de Beaugoin.
2 Mlle. Dartois.
1 Mme. Le Normand.
1 M. de Finnel.
1 M. de Lange.
1 Mme. de Montlegiets.
1 Mme. de la Fargue.

1778

1 Duchess de Chartres.
1 Mme. de Teuilly.
1 M. de Saint-Priest, ambassador.
2 M. and Mme. Dailly.
2 M. and Mme. Domnival.
1 Mme. Monge.
1 Mme. Degéraudot.
1 Marquis de Cossé.
1 Marquis d'Armaillé.
1 Duke de Cossé.
1 Mlle. de Ponse.
1 Monsieur, the King's brother.
1 Marquise de Montemey.
1 Mme. de Foissy.
2 The Brongniart children.
1 M. de Rannomanovski.
1 Mme. de Roissy.
1 Mme. de Bec de Lièvre.
1 Copy of portrait of the Queen.
2 Madame, wife of Monsieur.
1 Copy of portrait of Mme. Du Barry.
1 Mlle. Lamoignon.
1 Head of Mme. Vigée Lebrun.
1 Copy of portrait of Marie Antoinette.
1 Mme. Filorier.

1779

1 Marquis de Vrague.
1 Countess de Virieu.
1 Mme. Richard.
1 Mme. de Mongé.
1 Large portrait of the Queen for the Empress of Russia.
2 Half-length portraits of Marie Antoinette.
2 Copies of the same.
1 Mme. de Savigny.
2 The same with her son.
2 M. and Mme. de Lastic.
1 Woman as a Jewess for M. de Cossé.
1 Mme. Dicbrie.
2 Copies of busts of Marie Antoinette.
2 Mme. Ducluzel.
1 Mme. de Verdun.

1 Count de Dorsen, the younger.
2 M. and Mme. de Montesquiou.
1 Portrait of the Queen, for M. de Sartines.
1 Mme. de Palerme.
1 A little American.
1 Mlle. de la Ferté.
1 Head, looking down, for M. de Cossé.
1 Duke d'Orléans.
1 Marquise de Montesson.
2 Copies of the Duke d'Orléans.
2 Copies of large portrait of Marie Antoinette for M. de Vergennes.
1 Mme de Vannes.
1 Countess de Tournon.
1 Prince de Montbarrey.

1780

1 Mme. Lessout.
1 Large picture of Marie Antoinette.
1 The same.
4 Mme. de Verdun and family.
1 Mme. de Montesquiou.
1 Mme. de Montaudran.
1 Mme. Foulquier.
2 Mme. Genty.
1 Duchess de Mazarin

1781

1 Young girl smelling a rose.
1 Mme. Young.
1 Count de Cossé.
1 Princess de Croyes.
1 Mme. de Saint-Alban.
1 M. de Landry.
2 Portraits of Mme. Vigée Lebrun.
1 Monsieur, brother of the King.
1 Copy of same.
1 Duchess de Chaulnes.
1 Mme. Dumoley.
1 M. Dumoley, the younger.
1 Countess Du Barry.
1 Sketch for a picture of Juno.
1 Venus, study of a head.
1 Mme. d'Harvelay.
5 Studies of heads.
2 Mlle. de Laborde.
1 Mlle. Devaron.
1 Mme. Moreton.
1 Copy of M. Moreton.
1 Mme. de la Porte.
3 Princess Lamballe.

1782

1 Madame, sister of the King.
1 Copy of same.
1 Duchess de Polignac.
1 Copy of same.
1 Baron de Montesquiou.
1 Mme. de Verdun.
1 Mme. de Chatenay.
3 Prince Henry of Prussia.

1783

1 Marquise de la Guiche.
1 Mme. Grant.
1 Landgrave de Salm.
1 Mme. de Mailly.
2 Countess d'Artois.
2 Countess de Simiane.
2 Duchess de Guiche.
1 Marie Antoinette with hat.
2 The same in full dress.
2 Mme. Elisabeth, sister of the King.
1 Copy of same.
1 Mlle. Lavigne.
3 Copies of the Queen with hat.
4 The Queen in velvet dress.
4 Copies of same.
1 The Dauphin.
1 Mme. Royale, daughter of the King.

1784

1 Count de Vaudreuil.
5 Copies of same.
1 Countess de Grammont-Caderousse.
1 Countess de Serre.
1 M. de Beaujon.

1785

1 M. de Beaujon.
1 Princess de Carignan.
1 Mme. Fodi.
1 M. de Calonne.
1 Countess de Ségur.
1 Copy of same.
1 Count de Ségur.
1 Copy of same.
1 Baroness de Crussol.

1 M. de Saint-Hermine.
1 Grétry.
1 Countess de Clermont-Tonerre.
1 Countess de Virieu.
1 Viscountess de Vaudreuil.
2 Copies of the Queen in full dress.
1 Mme. Vigée.
1 Copy of M. de Calonne.
1 M. de Beaujon.

1786

1 Mme. Fouquet's little daughter.
1 Mme. de Tott.
1 Little d'Espagnac.
1 Mme. de la Briche's little daughter.
1 Mme. de Puységur.
1 Mme. Raymond.
1 Mme. Daudelot.
1 Mme. Davaray.
1 Countess de Sabran.
1 Mme. Vigée Lebrun and her daughter.

1787

1 Mlle. Lebrun reading the Bible.
1 Mme. de Rougé and two sons.
1 Mme. Dugazon, as *Nina*.
1 Cailleau, as a huntsman.
2 His two children.
1 Mlle. Lebrun in profile.
1 The same, looking at a mirror.
1 Mme. de la Grange.
1 Marie Antoinette and her children.
1 Mme. Vigée Lebrun.
2 Countess de Béon.
1 M. Le Jeune.
3 The Dauphin, Madame, and the Duke de Normandie.
1 Aunt of Mme. Verdun.
1 Duchess de Guiche, holding a wreath of flowers.
1 Pastel of same.
2 Duchess de Polignac with straw hat.
1 The same, singing at a piano.
1 Mme. de Chatenay.
1 Mme. Du Barry, full-length.
1 The same, in dressing-gown.
1 Mme. de Polignac.

1788

1 Duke de Polignac.
1 His father.
1 Robert, landscape painter.

1 Mme. Dumoley.
1 Mme. de la Briche.
1 Countess de Beaumont.
1 Little Baron d'Escars.
1 Little Prince Lubomirski.
1 The same, in pursuit of fame.
1 Little Brongniart.
1 Marquise de Grollier.
1 Le Bailly de Crussol.
1 Mme. de la Guiche, as a dairymaid.
1 Count d'Angevilliers.

1789

1 M. de Chatelux, from memory.
1 The Duke de Normandie, full-length.
1 Mme. Péregaux.
1 Mme. de Ségur, profile.
1 Large portrait of Marie Antoinette for the Baron de Breteuil.
1 Duchess de la Rochefoucauld.
1 Cupid.
1 Duchess d'Orléans.
1 Mme. Vigée Lebrun and daughter, for M. d'Angevilliers.
1 Mme. de Grollier.
1 Le Bailly de Crussol.
1 Mme. d'Aumont.
2 Mme. de Polignac.
2 Mme. de Guiche, pastel.
1 Mme. de Pienne.
1 Mme. de Châtre.
1 Mme. de Fresne-d'Aguesseau.
1 Marshal de Ségur.
1 Madame and the Dauphin.
1 Robert, the landscape painter.
1 Mlle. Lebrun, small oval.
1 Mme. Chalgrin.
1 Mme. Vigée Lebrun, pastel.
1 Joseph Vernet.
1 Prince of Nassau, full-length.
1 Mme. Vigée Lebrun, with daughter in arms.
1 Mme. Raymond with her child.
2 Mme. de Simiane.
2 Mme. Rousseau.
1 Mme. Duvernais.
1 Mme. de Saint-Alban.
1 Mme. Savigni.
1 Mlle. Dorion.
1 Mme. Du Barry.

DONE AT ROME

1 Mme. Vigée Lebrun, for the Academy of Lucca.
1 The same for the gallery at Florence.
1 Copy of same, for Lord Bristol.

1 Miss Pitt.
1 Mlle. Roland.
1 Mme. Silva, a Portuguese.
1 Countess Potocka.
2 Princesses Adelaide and Victoria, House of Bourbon.

VARIOUS LANDSCAPES, OILS AND CRAYONS
DONE AT NAPLES

1 Countess Skavronska, three-quarter length.
2 The same, half-length.
1 Lady Hamilton, as a reclining bacchante.
1 The same, as a sibyl, full-length.
1 The same, as a bacchante dancing.
1 Head of the same as a sibyl.
1 Princess Maria Theresa, who married Emperor Francis II.
1 Princess Maria Louisa, who married the Grand Duke of Tuscany.
1 Princess Marie-Christine, of Naples.
1 Paesiello, composer.
1 Prince Resonico.
1 Lord Bristol, three-quarter length.
1 Bailiff of Litta.
1 Queen of Naples.
Studies of Vesuvius and several landscapes.

DONE AT TURIN AND OTHER PLACES

1 Head, in oils, for the Academy of Parma.
1 Small portrait for the Institute of Bologna.
1 Mme. de Gourbillon.
1 Her son.
1 Mlle. Lebrun, as a bather.
1 Mlle. Porporati.
1 Copy of portrait of Raphael at Florence.
Various landscapes from nature.

DONE AT VENICE

1 Mme. Marini.

DONE AT VIENNA

1 Mme. Bistri, a Pole.
1 Mlle. de Caquenet.
1 Countess Kinska, three-quarter length.
1 The same, half-length.
1 Countess de Buquoi.
1 Countess Rasomovska.
1 Countess Palfi.
1 Princess Lichtenstein.

1 Count Strogonoff, half-length.
1 The same, hands showing.
1 Count Czernicheff, in black domino.
1 Countess Zamoiska, dancing.
1 Young Countess de Fries as Sapho.
1 Duchess de Guiche in blue turban.
2 Portraits of Prince Schotorinski, one with cloak.
1 Mme. de Schœnfeld, wife of Saxon Minister, with her child.
1 Prince Henry Lubomirski, playing on a lyre, with two naiades
    listening.
1 Princess Lichtenstein, as Iris.
1 Princess Esterhazy, sitting by the sea.
1 Princess Louise Galitzin.
1 Mme. Mayer.
1 Little girl bathing.
1 Countess Severin Potocka.
1 Princess of Wurtemberg.
1 Small picture for Count Wilsech.
1 Countess de Braonne, to the knees.
1 Small portrait for Mme. de Carpeny.
1 Duchess de Polignac, from memory, after her death.
1 Young Edmund de Polignac.
1 Princess Sapieha.

PASTELS DONE AT VIENNA

1 Count Woina, son of the Polish Ambassador.
1 Mlle. Caroline Woina, his sister.
1 Young Countess Metzy de Polignac.
1 Young Countess Thérèse de Hardik.
2 The two brothers of the Duchess de Guiche.
1 Brother of Mlle. de Fries, half-length.
2 Countess de Rombec, half-length.
1 Count Julius de Polignac.
1 Princess Linovska.
1 Lady Gaisford.
1 The de Choisy sisters.
1 Mlle. Schoen.
1 Agenor, infant son of the Duchess de Polignac.
1 His brother, Count de Fries.
1 Countess de Thun.
1 Countess d'Harrack.
1 Small drawing of the same
1 M. de Rivière.
1 M. Thomas, architect.
1 Countess de Rombec.
1 Marquis de Rivière.
    Landscapes near Vienna, from nature.

DONE IN RUSSIA

1 Mme. Dimidoff.
1 Princess Mentchikoff, with her child, three-quarter length.

1 Countess Potocka, with dove, reclining.
1 Young Countess Schouvaloff, half-length.
1 The young Grand Duchesses Helen and Alexandrina.
2 Grand Duchess Elizabeth, arranging flowers in a basket.
2 Half-length copies of the same.
2 Half-length pictures of her, one hand showing.
1 Countess Orloff.
1 Marshall Soltikoff.
2 Grand Duchess Anne, half-length.
2 Countess Scavronska, copied from portrait done at Naples.
1 Countess Strogonoff, with her child.
1 Count Strogonoff, half-length.
4 Countess Sammakloff, with her children.
1 Countess Apraxin.
1 Princess Isoupoff.
1 Her son.
2 Countess Voranxoff.
1 Countess Golovin, one hand showing.
1 Countess Tolstoï, leaning against a rock.
2 Princess Alexis Kurakin and her husband.
2 King Stanislaus Augustus Poniatowski, one in Henry IV. costume,
   the other in velvet cloak.
1 His great-niece, playing with a little dog.
1 Princess Michael Galitzin.
1 Emperor Alexander I., of Russia.
1 Empress Elizabeth, his wife.
1 Empress Maria of Russia, wife of the Emperor Paul.
2 Countess Diedrichstein and her husband.
1 Princess Bauris Galitzin, three-quarter length.
1 Lord Talbot, half-length.
1 Princess Sapieha, with tambour, dancing.
1 Daughter of Princess Isoupoff.
1 Mme. Kutusoff, half-length.
1 Baron Strogonoff.
1 Mlle. Kasisky.
1 Princess Alexander Galitzin.
1 Mme. Kalitcheff.
1 Count Potocka.
1 Count Litta.
1 Princess Viaminski.
1 Young Prince Bariatinski.
2 Prince Alexander Kurakin, half-length.
1 Mme. Vigée Lebrun, in black, to the knees, holding palette, for the
   Academy of St. Petersburg.

DONE AT BERLIN

2 Pastels of the Queen of Prussia.
1 Mme. de Souza, Portuguese Ambassadress.
1 Portrait of a lady.

DONE AT DRESDEN

3 Emperor Alexander, copied from portrait done at St. Petersburg.
1 Daughter of the Countess Potocka.
1 A German lady.

DONE IN ENGLAND

1 Miss Dorset.
1 Mme. Chinnery.
2 Her children.
1 Miss Dillon.
1 Mme. Villiers.
1 Margravine of Anspach.
1 Mme. Baring.
1 Prince of Wales.
1 Mme. de Polastron.
1 Countess Diedrichstein.
2 Infant son of Mme. de Polastron
1 Lord Byron.
1 Prince Bariatinski.
1 An American lady.
1 Son of Margravine of Anspach.
3 Portraits of Mme. Vigée Lebrun.
3 Mme. Grassini, two of them in oriental costume, the other half-length.
1 Portrait of an Irish lady.
1 Lady Georgina, daughter of Lady Gordon.
1 Prince Biron of Courland, as a huntsman.
1 Two sons of Countess de Vaudreuil.
Views of the seacoast in crayons, and several landscapes.

DONE AT PARIS AFTER RETURNING

1 Queen of Prussia, from picture done at Berlin, large half-length.
1 Prince Ferdinand of Prussia.
1 Prince Augustus Ferdinand, his son.
1 Princess Louise Radzivill, his sister.
1 Princess Tufakin.
1 Mme. Catalani, singing at a piano.
1 Mme. Murat, with her daughter.
4 Portraits of Mme. Vigée Lebrun for friends.
3 Mme. Grassini.
1 M. Ragani, her husband.
1 Viscountess de Vaudreuil.
2 Count de Vaudreuil, her uncle.
2 Duchess de Guiche.
1 Young Princess Potemski, half-length.
1 Mme. Constans.
1 Countess d'Andlau, with hands showing.
1 Duke de Berri.
2 Countess de Rosambeau and Countess d'Orglande, daughters of Countess d'Andlau.
2 The two d'Andlau brothers.
1 Viotti, famous violinist.
1 Marquise de Grollier, painting flowers.
1 M. de Crussol, large half-length picture.
1 Mlle. de Grénonville.
1 Mme. Davidoff.

1 Marquis de Rivière, for King Charles X., half-length.
1 Count de Coëtlosquet.
1 Mme. de Pront, his niece
2 Duchess de Berri.
1 Mlle. de Sassenay.
1 M. Raoul Rochette.
1 M. Sapey.
1 Mme. Lafont.
1 Mlle. de Rivière.
1 Alfred de Rivière.
1 Baron de Feisthamel, painting.
1 Baron de Crespy le Prince, drawing.
1 Mme. Ditte.
1 Mme. de Rivière, both hands showing.
1 Profile of Mme. Vigée Lebrun, for a medallion for the City of St. Petersburg, on which Angelica Kauffman was also to appear.

SUNDRY PICTURES

1 Poetry, Painting and Music.
1 Spanish Scene.
1 Love asleep under a tree.
1 Young girl, surprised in her shirt
1 Young girl, caught writing.
1 Innocence seeking refuge in the arms of Justice.
1 Venus binding the wings of Love.
1 Juno asking girdle from Venus.
1 Bacchante with tiger-skin.
1 Peace bringing back Plenty.
1 Apotheosis of the Queen.
1 Shipwrecked woman.
1 Cataract of Narva.
1 Amphion playing on the lyre.
1 An old man with his son.
About 200 Swiss and English landscapes.

SUNDRY PORTRAITS

1 Mme. Ducrest de Villeneuve.
1 Marquise de Jancourt.
1 Countess de Provence.
1 Woman painting.
1 Mme. Molé-Raymond, of the Comédie-Française, with muff.
1 The infant Duke de Berri.
1 Lady playing the harp.
1 Countess Czartoryska.
1 Mme. Courcelles.
1 Davich Khan.
1 His son.
1 Prince de Rochefort.
1 Cardinal Fleury, from an engraving.
1 La Bruyère, from an engraving.
1 Mme. de Suffrein, from memory.
1 Abbé Delille, from memory.
1 Countess de Las Casas, from memory.

INDEX